READER REVIEWS

The following are reviews by readers who acquired copies of the first and second printing of this book:

I recently read Fred Nashed's An Ancient Egyptian in Texas and found it a good read. I especially liked how he covered some of the early history of modern day Egypt and his description of his growing up as a Christian in a Moslem country. His tales of some of the misadventures he had as an immigrant living in Texas were both heart warming and humorous. I gave my copy to my immigrant daughter-in-law and she said she delighted in reading the book and remembering some of the experiences trying to fit in her new surroundings very similar to what Fred experienced. Autobiographies are not my reading choice, I find them to be, as a rule, self-serving, but this book is an exception.I highly recommend it.
Andrea Martin, 2010.

Wonderfully written an insight look into life in Egypt. Tells it like it is.
David Lopez, 2013.

Mr. Nashed tells us a warm story of love and luck. He makes abundantly clear that he (and we) are so very lucky to have our freedom, our love and our God. I found the book to be most interesting and satisfying. Fred's ability to use mundane struggles to provide a really 'good read' is most remarkable. Welcome to the 'good old USA', Fred.
Dan Heather, 2013.

AN ANCIENT EGYPTIAN IN TEXAS

FRED NASHED

This book was first published by VBW
in 2010. It was then republished by
CreateSpace in 2013. The current
version was amended and added to.

ACKNOWLEDGMENTS

The author wishes to acknowledge the laborious efforts his wife, Gayle, made in repeatedly reviewing Part 2 of this text, amending the sequence of events and adding many details he had forgotten. She also collaborated in reviewing and amending this iteration. He also wishes to thank the remaining members of his family for providing information, insights and corrections that were invaluable for rounding out Part 1 of the book. Thanks are also due to our friend Connie Timko who used her photographic skills to take the final picture in this text.

Special thanks to Jenny Meadows, my copy editor, who checked the text of the last two versions and made improvements in the structure and flow of the narrative. The enthusiasm, dedication and diligence she brought to bear on this autobiography to make sure that it was as near perfect as humanly possible is deeply appreciated. The current edition was proof-read by Gayle Nashed (nee: Gayle Lynette Hensley).

To my beloved wife Gayle whose support and help were invaluable to this effort and throughout my life after I came to the States.

CONTENTS

FORWARD

Three dead goldfish! Not a pretty picture but it was the turning point from friendship to a growing love of the Ancient Egyptian I had met only months earlier. I was living in Andrews Dorm at the University of Texas and prized my three fancy-tailed goldfish that lived in a big glass jar with colored glass at the bottom and green water plants for them to swim through. I loved watching them as a break from studying. Over the Thanksgiving weekend, I left them with a friend since I was riding the bus home for the holiday. With strict instructions on how to feed them, I thought their well-being was assured for the four day period. Wrong! When I returned, there they were floating on the surface of a green algae-filled container. I was devastated. I called Fouad (he later adopted the name Fred) and he took the situation as seriously as I felt it required and said he would be right over, He helped me bury them at the base of a large loquat tree in the dorm quadrangle. And then he went a step further and offered to take me to buy new ones! Not once did he say, "Good grief, they were only goldfish or "Just flush them down the toilet." And only later did I understand how trivial dead goldfish must have appeared to someone who had come from a country where, when I later visited, I saw children with their families digging through heaps of garbage scrounging whatever they could find to sell to eke out a living. I was overwhelmed by how cheap human life was in Egypt and yet he had made the switch and understood that dead goldfish were important to me at that time. I loved him then and even more after seeing and understanding better the poverty and hardship that surrounded him in the country where he grew up.

I entered this man's life when he was 39 years old and I was 21 soon to be 22, a milestone in the lives of most U.S. youth. He sent me flowers and I was blown away already knowing how limited his finances were. We were more friends than boyfriend/ girlfriend at the start. Fouad was so curious about everything from foods in the grocery store to what made a woman tick. He was a culture sponge asking about things we in the U.S. just assume to be true, right or just the way they are. The innate teacher in me loved telling him about the whys, hows and wherefores. And I loved listening to his stories about a country so totally different from mine. Yet, we quickly found that our own families were very much alike, teaching frugality, self-reliance, the importance of one's word and punctuality, a trait that is rather rare in the Middle East! And while my polio disability seemed to be disconcerting to him at first since the handicapped in Egypt are relegated to the background of society, he adapted or I should say he analyzed the situation and found I had other redeeming factors! "Analyze it" is his way of dealing with challenges and he uses this method to make decisions of all kinds. And once I was diagnosed with Post-Polio Syndrome, a re-weakening of those limbs (in my case mainly my right leg), that were initially affected by the virus, he put that analyzing ability to work on how to keep me as independent and engaged as possible in the things we enjoy. First, when he saw how exhausted I was at the end of the day especially when travelling -which we liked and still like to do- he suggested getting a wheelchair to lessen the physical stress of long walks, especially on uneven surfaces in Europe. Since I am more emotional than analytical, I reacted with tears and felt it was a step backward for me who had spent years struggling to be "normal" in spite of a limp. However, his patient convincing argument won out, the wheelchair was bought and we continued to enjoy our travels. Then when pushing me became less easy for him, he spent hours online researching mobility scooters and automatic lifts for our vehicle in an effort to keep me as mobile as possible and to enable us to continue to visit new and interesting places. When the small red Go-Go scooter entered our world, he once again analyzed the situation and found that in order for him to keep up with the speed and distance I could now cover plus the fun I was having zooming about, he needed a vehicle of his own. So he came up with the idea of attaching a small companion wheelchair to the back of the scooter so I could tow him. Much to the delight and amusement of people in Chicago, Washington, D.C., Seattle, Ft. Fort and ports of call during several cruises, we have had great fun in our "combo scooter train". We covered so much of Chicago in our contraption while spending a week there, one of the bus drivers who picked us up at the stop near our hotel said, "Oh, yeah, I have seen you two all over town!" We continue to get thumbs up, "that's the way to go", "can we hook up behind you" and "that is so clever" from those we pass wherever we go especially after a long and busy day at Disney World, one of our favorite places to vacation.

And now I have a confession to make -- there has been another man in our lives all these years, Frank Lloyd Wright, the well-known architect. It wasn't long after I got to know Fouad when he introduced me to Frank and he has been around since then. Frank has come into our home through several books, videos and now the internet. His architecture is the gold standard in Fouad's view by which all else is measured and discussed. Every building we enter is taken apart and compared to Frank's concepts and designs. We visited Taliesin West and enjoyed hearing about the deeds and misdeeds of Mr. Wright as he is called there. Of course we knew much of what we heard from reading and seeing presentations about his work and life but being in a building where he walked was an entirely different experience. Of course we brought home several examples of his design to display – just a reminder that Frank, oh, excuse me, Mr. Wright is always near!

Fouad is also a man of strong faith, a Christian, but not one to get hung up on denominations. An Orthodox Copt in Egypt but because I was "conceived" a Lutheran, he readily joined my church after we got married. His faith gave him the strength to leave his family and start a new life in the U.S. at an age when most men have settled comfortably into their careers. He trusted that God would be with him and help him start anew. He looks at each twist of his life and clearly sees the work of God at every turn. Fouad speaks easily about how he came to know Jesus and has had conversations with those he has met on cruises as well as with his own brothers. He cites John, his favorite book of the Bible, as being so authentic only someone who was there to see the story unfold could have written it. He is not one to use the name of Jesus in every sentence but, a quiet and strong believer who sees the works of God in everyday life.

And what a blessing Fouad has been to me! I have always told him that I prayed for someone like him to share my life without really even knowing what that person might be like. A man with a good sense of humor, a man with a bit of silliness that escapes from time to time, a man who took our marriage vow as seriously as I did, a man who is a hard worker, a man who is not afraid to learn new things like using a computer in his mid-70's and a man that has made every day an adventure for me. He took a young small-town Texan and showed her the world!

Gayle H. Nashed,

PART 1

EGYPT FOR ROMANCE

INTRODUCTION

I consider myself an Ancient Egyptian, not literally but by ancestry. Here is how: I was born in Egypt in a Coptic (Christian) family descended from the Ancient Egyptians. The long history of Egypt started in 3000 BC (more than 5000 years ago) with a population that eventually developed a sophisticated culture which produced the pyramids and the famous temples that, until recently, were visited by millions of tourists every year. Their society lasted for many centuries. The Greeks under Alexander the Great conquered the country, intermarried with the local population and ruled for a long time. The country was then conquered by the Romans who remained for a shorter period, during which Christianity was introduced by St. Mark to a Jewish community in Alexandria and the new religion spread to the Greco-Egyptian population from which my family was descended much later. My green eyes and those of others in my family attest to some Roman or Greek blood in our ancestry as well. After the Arabs invaded in 639 AD, Christians remained faithful to their beliefs before the Moslem Arabs gave them three choices: convert to Islam, pay a confiscatory tax or be executed. In spite of this, many either paid the taxes or accepted death rather than recant (Does this remind the reader of what is currently happening in the Middle East and elsewhere?). This autobiography's title is based on that synopsis of history.

Many people may wonder what makes someone leave his native land, his family, his friends, and everything that is familiar to him to start a new life where he doesn't know anybody and is not totally familiar with the customs of the people or the nuances of the language of another country. This account, which is based on my actual experiences, answers that question. It explains why this seemingly illogical behavior occurred in my case. It elaborates on my travails in Egypt, my first years in my adopted country, my joys and disappointments. It also mentions the wonderful opportunities that enabled me to establish a comfortable life in my new homeland with the loving assistance of Gayle, my adorable American wife.

Part 1 of the book presents interesting and sometimes shocking facts about the culture and a partial history of modern Egypt, a unique description of daily life in Cairo and the experiences of my family. It will touch on my schooling and how I experienced discrimination as a child and in high school. It ends with what I went through as a government employee and how God enabled me to leave the country against all odds. I was the third and last of my brothers to immigrate. It is important to point out that my life there was not devoid of enjoyment. It was only when I started to realize that I had no future there and working conditions had become akin to serfdom that I finally decided to make a drastic change by immigrating to the U.S. at the ripe old age of 38.

Part 2 describes my elation at being successful in my efforts to leave the country to start my life in the United States and enjoy the freedoms and opportunities that were denied me in Egypt, how I supported myself on the $200 that the Egyptian government allowed immigrants to take out of the country, and how I thrived in graduate school. It explains the circumstances under which I met a fascinating girl who eventually agreed to become my wife and made me a very happy man, and how my career evolved until I started my own consulting business, became an author and retired to a wonderful active-adult community where everybody is friendly and life is delightful. This autobiography is intended for those who are contemplating making the agonizing decision to immigrate. It is also intended for those who like to read human-interest stories which attest to God's grace.

Chapter 1
EGYPTIAN SOCIETY AND CULTURE

My wife, Gayle, and I are sitting on the back porch sipping fresh-brewed coffee, enjoying the view of our exquisitely landscaped rock garden and watching the hummingbirds visiting every flower and fighting each other for the privilege. The setting sun is painting the clouds a gorgeous reddish color. It is a magical moment of sheer contentment, and I feel a wave of gratitude to God and this country for providing such a wonderful and secure haven for a stranger like me. I remember my journey from the time I landed in New York with less than $200 in my pocket until I achieved all my aspirations, writing books and becoming an independent consultant dealing with architectural technology, and all the opportunities that led to that moment on the terrace. I could not help but hark back to my life in Egypt, the country where I was born and where I spent the first thirty-eight years of my life.

To give an idea about the prevailing conditions surrounding my life then, I will describe the society and culture of my former country which may be totally different from the one that the reader is accustomed to. While I lived there, "EGYPT FOR ROMANCE" was the heading on all English-language tourism posters displayed in many public spaces and in magazine ads targeting foreign tourists. In our family it was a laughable slogan; whenever something went wrong, we rolled our eyes and said, "Egypt for Romance," to express disgust and disbelief. You see, that slogan does not apply to Egyptians because Egypt had extreme restrictions on the display of affection between the sexes in public. In fact, there was a special police unit called the "Morals Police" tasked with intervening if they suspected a couple of fraternizing, kissing, holding hands or even walking together in public. We could not perceive how romance could survive under such circumstances. Using this statement to represent the country was the height of hypocrisy since one had to conform to the norm of allowing encounters between the sexes only in the presence of a chaperone.

The country had a stratified society divided along distinct classes. Peasants and laborers were, on the whole, uneducated and considered lower-class people with very low wages and limited rights which were often ignored. They lived in old, substandard housing in poor neighborhoods which, in many cases, were illegally built and, by consequence, illegally connected to utilities. Some, mostly poor Christians, worked collecting garbage and recycling it. In some cases, they lived illegally in old abandoned mausoleums in cemeteries. Most people belonging to that class accepted their lot without complaining.

The middle class, to which our family belonged, was educated, received better pay (though puny by Western standards), enjoyed some non-essentials, rented apartments located in better parts of the city paying affordable rents. They performed clerical and professional work. They also engaged in commerce and construction. If they succeeded, they became well-to-do and became capable of overcoming most obstacles by bribing the bureaucrats who created obstacles to earn those bribes. The Christians among them confronted many difficulties when they tried to engage in commerce or entrepreneurial work, as will be described later in the text.

The upper-class included the rich landed gentry and politicians with Turkish titles, such as *Bey* and *Pasha* bestowed by the king, usually after a transfer of a large sum of money to an aide to the king. That class had influence, owned their residences, enjoyed luxuries and either drove cars or were chauffeured to their destinations. Those titles were abolished when King Farouk, the last king to sit on the throne, was deposed in 1951.

Religion

Islam is the official religion of the country. The overwhelming majority belong to the Sunni sect. Mosques are ubiquitous. During my childhood, the *Imam* who led the prayers would go up into the minaret (mosque tower) to call the faithful to prayer five times a day. These sing-song calls sounded dreamy and added to the charm of the city. One day, an innovative and lazy *Imam* (prayer leader) discovered the magic of loud speakers, probably because they saved him from having to climb the arduous spiral staircase within the minaret. As a result, the city changed overnight with the loud, echoing calls sounding from minarets far and near. It definitely impacted the quality of life and made all those who did not belong to Islam rather uncomfortable.

Many Americans assume that Christianity was introduced by missionaries to the country. Copts, a sect of Orthodox Christianity unique to Egypt and Ethiopia, believe that St. Mark introduced Christianity to a Jewish synagogue in Alexandria (which was the capital at that time) around 42 AD. Centuries later, missionaries were able to convert a small percentage to Catholicism and Protestantism. The majority of Egyptians became Christian during the rule of Roman Emperor Justinian. After the Arabs invaded in 639 AD, Christians remained faithful to their beliefs; however, due to persecutions and the imposition of a heavy tax called *Al djizya* which deprived them of a big chunk of their income, a large number were eventually forced to convert to Islam to avoid being killed or becoming destitute.

Al djizya was imposed under the pretext that it was to cover the costs of defending the Christians against invaders (something that never happened) since they were forbidden by the government from joining the army. Moslems, of course, were exempt from that tax. When the Moslem *Mameluks* (freed slaves of the Turks) took charge of the country after the fall of the Ottoman Empire which had ruled the country, they increased the persecution and brutal torture of Christians. The result was that the majority converted to Islam in the twelfth century AD. The *djizya* was finally lifted in the 19th century.

Legend has it that when persecution reached an intolerable level, Al Mokowkus, the leader of the Copts, sent a comely maiden to the Prophet Mohammad as a plea to ease up on them. The prophet added her to his harem and, in response, sent a message to the Moslem ruler of Egypt recommending that the Copts be treated kindly. To this day, there is a popular saying among Egyptian Moslems when they are rebuked for receiving a bribe. It goes something like this: "Since even the Prophet himself accepted the present, who am I to refuse a gift?" What is implied is that the Prophet, in his exalted position as the emissary of Allah, accepted a present to modify his policy. Some Christians held on to their faith, in spite of all that persecution. My parents' ancestors were among those hardy souls. Today, the Christian minority represents around 10% (about 8.2 million) of a population of 82 million (today the population is estimated to be at 92 million). The government census alleges that they represent only 6% to trivialize their importance and deny them representation in its parliament.

The majority of Christians belong to the Coptic Orthodox Church with a small percentage belonging to the other denominations. During my childhood, Coptic priests in the church I sporadically attended had limited education and their sermons were singularly uninteresting. They shed no light on the scriptures but restated them without adding any clarifications to enlighten or inspire the congregation. They expected people to kiss their hand and treat them with extreme respect, which people did, in spite of the fact that nothing in the scripture required them to do so. This custom was humiliating and unwarranted. I remember once when the priest extended his hand to my sister Hilda, she took it, turned it over and kissed the back of her own hand; a clever maneuver to avoid having to kiss his. I remember hearing a joke about one of those sermons which went something like this: "Jesus saw Zaccharias perched on a tree and He told him, 'Zacchaeus, come down from the tree.' Did He say, 'Descend from the tree'? No, He said, 'Come down.' Did He say, 'Stay up there'? No, He said, 'Come down.' See the wisdom of God." My sister Laura told me recently that things have improved since I left. Now priests have to be college graduates before being tapped for the priesthood.

It was only in my twenties when life became really tough that I was led by the Spirit to believe, after reading the King James Bible according to the apostle John as well as the Acts of the Apostles. I found the narrative to be so realistic, I concluded that no writer at that early time could have made up all the details of these wonderful accounts. After that I started attending a Protestant service frequented by members of the American Embassy. It was conducted in English, a language I was familiar with. The service was well-organized and lasted only an hour as opposed to the three hours at the Coptic service. The choir was melodious and the attendees were friendly though not overly welcoming to Egyptians. I think they may have suspected that most of the locals were spies appointed by the Egyptian government to check the sermon. Their suspicions might have been well-founded, because the government had secret agents everywhere. They cost so little to employ.

Jews represented a relatively small minority in Egypt when I lived there and, in spite of the fact that Jews have lived in Alexandria since biblical times, President Nasser ousted them after hostilities broke out with England, France and Israel when he nationalized the Suez Canal. He also, ousted all European citizens including Italians and British nationals. In our apartment building almost half the apartments were occupied by Jewish families who had to evacuate in a hurry as a result of a hasty order by the government to leave the country. My brother, who still lives in Egypt, told me recently some Israelis now spend their vacations snorkeling in Horgada, a resort on the Red Sea, as a result of the treaty between Egypt and Israel which was brokered by President Carter during President Anwar Sadat's rule. I will elaborate on that episode later.

Education
Education was organized by the British who were in charge of the government at the time. They had labeled Egypt as a protectorate after ousting the French who had occupied it briefly during Napoleon's conquests. Under the British system, students started with four years of primary school followed by five years of secondary school after which a rigorous, nationwide final exam had to be passed before a student became eligible to apply for admittance to the university (there was only one university at the time). English was taught in both primary and secondary schools and French in secondary school only. Religious classes were split in primary school. Christian students attended a class taught by a Coptic teacher, and

Moslem students attended another taught by a Moslem teacher. Most schools were run by the government, however, a few were parochial schools run by Copts or Jews. The parochial schools occupied older buildings and were not as well equipped or funded as government schools. Girls attended separate schools. Some, like the French Lycée, the English School and the British Victoria College, were more expensive private schools.

Cairo

Cairo is the capital of Egypt. Its population today is more than 8 million (17+ million in the metropolitan area) and growing rapidly. In 1968, the last year I lived there, its population was 4 million. The city is very hot in summer and the sun heated the flat concrete roof slab above our apartment and caused it to act as a radiator. It was awful. With no air-conditioning in those days, one just closed the shutters, sweated and learned to live with it. Tap water was stored in *olla*s, clay jug-shaped pots which sweated through their pores, keeping the surface of the vessel damp. The breeze evaporated the water and, in so doing, lowered the temperature of the contents, keeping it at an optimum temperature for drinking. It was our ecological way of cooling water. I suspect that those *olla*s were introduced by the Ancient Egyptians. Fortunately our family didn't have to spend the hot months of June, July and August in Cairo. During that time my parents took us to Alexandria, the second largest city in Egypt, to spend our school vacation swimming in the Mediterranean and enjoying the fun.

Cairo today (note the smog)

Cairo radio, at the time of the British occupation during WWII, had a station that targeted teen-agers, foreign nationals, tourists and the British military personnel stationed there. It broadcast programs in English which included British and American songs in a call-in program entitled, "At Your Request". It included French, Italian and, of course, Arabic songs (the language of the country). At age five, I listened to both Arabic and western music and found that I preferred the latter so I stuck with it for the rest of my life. I had the same feelings about movies. After I watched a couple of Egyptian films, I found that they covered only one subject, romantic love, which was something I wasn't interested in as a child. On the other hand, western movies, especially American ones, included adventure, shoot'em ups, comedies and war movies. Egyptian films did not compare even remotely to the quality and variety of American movies. We used to buy roasted and salted squash seeds packaged in funnel-shaped recycled pieces of newspapers to consume during the show. They performed the same function as popcorn here.

Traffic

During the time that I was growing up, Cairo was a nice city to live in, traffic was well-controlled because only a few people owned cars. While the four million people living there before I emigrated made it a relatively large city, it was livable. Today, at seventeen million and growing, nothing seems to work. The lines demarcating street lanes are considered as decoration and drivers straddle them at will. Traffic lights are regarded as optional recommendations and you take your life in your hands if you decide to cross the street. Horse or donkey-drawn carts mingle with cars and buses, adding to the chaos. The car horn is the most important piece of equipment on the vehicle and it is used liberally, creating an insufferable cacophony! The sidewalks are so crowded one almost has to make reservations to use them. The air is more polluted due to the ever increasing number of cars.

Society

While I was growing up during the thirties and forties, our apartment overlooked a lively street. Hawkers pushing handcarts shouted a description of their wares in sing-song incantations. Those descriptions ranged from the mundane such as *"Elaal ya batatess,"* meaning "fantastic potatoes!" to the fanciful such as *"Elkoosa hashwa zibdaaa,"* meaning "The squash is stuffed with butter" (of course it was just ordinary squash). When my widowed sister Hilda and her two sons were living with me in the family apartment after everybody else had either gotten married, died or immigrated, her older son, Samir (two years old and just learning to talk), heard all those hawkers and created an imaginary call, believing it meant something. He would toddle around the apartment shouting, *"El labaleya b'ersh, el labaleya b'ersh!"* Meaning "the *labaleya* (a word of his own invention) is for one piaster" (piaster is a common coin equivalent to about 20 cents). He said it with such gusto, it made us laugh. I have no idea whether hawkers still exist today or not.

From time to time, a Moslem funeral would proceed down the street. The relatives and friends of the deceased would take turns carrying a crude open wooden box at a brisk pace. A green sheet covered the body of the deceased. They chanted the *Shehada* (testament) which went like this, "*La ilaha illalah, Mohammad rasulullah, sallalahu allahu alaih wa sallam,*" which, when translated, roughly meant "There is no God but Allah and Mohammad is his prophet the blessed by Allah." They repeated this over and over all the way to the cemetery. Sometimes veiled women wearing black, all-enveloping garments would follow, wailing and saying things such as, "You who died before eating your favorite kebab" or some other dish. They were professional wailers hired by the family to show the world how they loved and missed the deceased. Funerals for Christians were more subdued and evinced real grief and tears in silence. An ornate casket would be transported ahead of the procession in a horse-drawn carriage.

That evening, if the Moslem deceased had lived in our neighborhood, our street would be blocked off by a special ornate fabric pavilion erected to receive the mourners. A loudspeaker was installed and passages from the Qur'an, the Moslem holy book, were intoned by a sheik to provide a background sound for those attending the reception. We had to live with that noise but we were accustomed to enduring the city-wide cacophony of loudspeakers calling worshipers to the mosques five times a day, including one at dawn. Apparently, those Qur'an passages did not have to do with death or consolation. I remember going to one of those affairs when a fellow architect's father died. I knew no one, so I listened to what the chanting sheik was broadcasting and noticed that the passage or *Sura* that he chose detailed how to perform the sexual act! A few days later, I told my fellow worker, whose father's funeral it was, about what I had heard and he said,

"That son of a dog. I will deal with him when I get home." In his grief and preoccupation with receiving the people who came to pay their respects, he hadn't been paying attention to what the sheik was saying and apparently no one else had either because they were too busy visiting.

Chapter 2
EGYPT'S RECENT HISTORY

A country's government has a profound effect on the lives of its citizens. Starting with the Pharaohs until the present, Egypt has been ruled by a kind of benign dictatorship. In this chapter, I will address only the country's history from the time I came on the scene in 1930 until I emigrated in 1968. King Fouad ruled while I was a kid. He died in 1936 and I watched his funeral procession from the flat rooftop of our apartment building. His funeral had all the pomp and circumstance befitting a monarch, complete with an honor guard and classic funerary music. He was followed by his son, King Farouk, whose government became deeply engulfed in favoritism and corruption. He was deposed in 1951 in a bloodless coup by army officers led by General Mohammad Naguib. Naguib was deposed by Colonel Nasser, who was elected president in 1954.

When the king moved between his palaces, he chose the weekend to get full exposure so the media would announce the event. Our family watched the procession from the window overlooking his route. It was quite a spectacle. First, the streets along the route were cleared of all traffic and police officers lined both sides at thirty-foot intervals. After the spectators waited for a while, a motorcycle officer blowing a whistle sped down the street. After another wait, another officer would repeat the procedure, then a third, heightening peoples' expectation. This was followed by two red vintage Rolls Royce cars transporting dignitaries, and next came the king in an open sedan of the same color. He graciously waved to the madly clapping crowds that lined the whole route. This was followed by a few more cars belonging to the procession and a few police motorcycles. After that, traffic would resume. Auto dealerships were forbidden from importing red cars into the country because it was the exclusive royal car color!

World War II
During WWII, while the Germans and Italians under General Rommel were advancing in Libya and Egypt's western desert, their Luftwaffe and the Italian Air Force conducted nightly air raids on Cairo, targeting the British military camps. A total blackout was imposed and Egyptian air-raid wardens blew whistles and yelled whenever somebody erroneously showed some light. Car owners had to paint their headlights dark blue. Some bombs missed their targets and fell on apartment buildings, killing civilians. It was a terrifying time for everybody. Windows had to be shuttered and their glass taped to prevent injury if it shattered. At the sound of the air-raid sirens, usually around two or three o'clock in the morning, our entire family was shocked into instant wakefulness and had to climb down twelve flights of stairs (three flights per story) to an occupied apartment on the first floor which was designated as an air-raid shelter. It was deemed safer because of its two-foot-thick exterior walls. We had to wait until the all-clear siren blared, declaring the end of the raid, then climb back up those nine flights. Sometimes another siren would sound a short while later and we had to do it all over again. On several occasions, it turned out to be a false alarm and nothing happened.

After going up and down countless times, my family, which was composed of nine children and two parents, decided to stay put in our fourth-floor apartment. The rationale was that if the building sustained a direct hit, it would collapse and bury those who were on the lower floors so, why bother? Whenever the alarm went off, we peered through the shutters and saw the search lights scanning the sky. Many-colored tracer shells rose from anti-aircraft guns until they reached a certain altitude and exploded with a pop. We also saw and heard the awesome distant flash and *"Krrrump"* sound of bombs exploding as well as anti-aircraft shells. At least we had an interesting show to watch instead of just hearing those awesome explosions while we quaked on the ground floor and having to do a strenuous exercise going up and down those stairs in the small hours of the morning.

The weekend following each raid, my brothers and I would tour the neighborhood and inspect the demolished buildings and, in some instances, blood stains from the victims who were taken to the hospital or morgue. Wilson, my eldest brother, said during one of these raids, "These explosions are drums." He went to the piano and, not knowing how to play, hit the keys at random. It was just a charade that produced an awful racket. I guess he wanted to distract us and calm our nerves as well as his own. On one occasion, a bomb fell through the roof of a public garage a block away. Fortunately, it did not explode but created a sizable hole in the metal roof and another deep hole in the floor of the garage. A British bomb-disposal team dug it up, defused it and took it away.

That incident inspired Wilson, who was a licenced pharmacist, to move the family during the summer to a safe village about 400 miles south of Cairo after he found a position at the local government-run hospital as a combination pharmacist/anesthesiologist. He used to regale us with stories about the horrors inflicted on the poor peasants that had to undergo surgery. The outcome was invariably death. He called the surgeons "butchers" because they were not interested in improving their knowledge or techniques. They considered these poor helpless peasants as expendable guinea pigs. I remember him describing a case of lock-jaw and another involving the opening up of a patient's abdomen because he had acute bowel blockage that had lasted a long time. Of course, the usual outcome resulted. It was nauseating for him to watch these potentially preventable deaths.

Living in the village

The village did not have running water, so a water carrier delivered water every day in a goatskin carried on his back to fill a tank located above the sink. It did not taste as good as Cairo water but, after a while, we got used to it. Each morning, my brother Sobhi and I went to the fields to pick the vegetables my mother would cook that day as well as for the salad. It was kind of fun for us kids (I was 10 or 11 years old and he was 5 years older). For the first time I saw where these familiar vegetables came from. While life in the village was primitive, it was also peaceful and away from the continuous air raids that terrorized us and robbed us of sleep. Living in the country was also healthier since the produce was always fresh and the air unpolluted. At the end of our summer vacation, we returned to our shuttered apartment and endured a few more air raids before the Germans and Italians were defeated by the Allies in El Alamain, a village not far from Alexandria.

War with Israel

A few years after the world war, the Egyptian government coordinated an attack on Israel with Syria and Jordan. A counterattack led by Moshe Dayan, a veteran Israeli general, defeated all three armies. A short time afterward, Egypt terminated an agreement which allowed Britain to occupy a huge military base that controlled the Suez Canal, a daring patriotic step to regain sovereignty. When the British did not vacate the base, guerillas attacked it and the government did not curb their efforts. The British retaliated by attacking a major police station, killing forty policemen, and the government was not able to defy the power of the British Empire. In retaliation, a fanatical group called the Moslem Brotherhood rampaged in Cairo, burning movie theaters, liquor stores, and foreign-owned businesses as well as killing foreigners, including ten British citizens. The group's avowed goal was to take over the government and impose *Shari'a* (Islamic law) on the country. That law included cutting off the hand of a thief, stoning women accused of adultery, beheading a murderer, reintroducing the *hejab* (veil) and declaring that Islamic law applies to everybody regardless of their religious affiliations. A grocery store located across the street from our apartment building was among their targets. It was owned by Mr. Christodoulou, a Greek whom we knew, and the smoke from that fire billowed to our apartment on the fourth story.

As a result of the defeat of the Egyptian armed forces at the hand of Israel and the turmoil created by the Moslem Brotherhood, a group of army officers plotted to depose King Farouk and take over the government. While the reign of King Farouk meant great separation between the classes in society and a bad example of a roué king under the hegemony of a British overlord, restrictions on personal freedoms were minimal for educated people. They could travel abroad any time they felt like it, whether for tourism or education. They could change jobs if they wanted to. Private enterprise was alive and well, regardless of the fact that it was canted in favor of the Moslems and impeded by the ever-present government corruption. Christians and Moslems lived generally in peace. In addition, inflation was under control and the standard of living was tolerable. This, however, started to change when the

Moslem Brotherhood fanatics came on the scene.

The Rise of Nasser

In 1952, the year I graduated from college, King Farouk was deposed in a bloodless coup. After a period of adjustment, the army officers who deposed him chose Colonel Gamal Abdel Nasser to lead the country. Nasser had a negative effect on my family. At the end of my senior year at the Faculty of Fine Arts, all hiring came to a grinding halt until political power sorted itself out. I applied for the position of architect at Cairo Municipality, but the hiring freeze remained for a full year. During that year of unemployment, I, along with my widowed sister and her two sons who shared the family apartment with me, eked out a living on the measly salary from my evening job and by receiving some assistance from my brothers, who helped us survive. Finally, I received a letter informing me I had been hired.

A few years after assuming power, Nasser decided to hold presidential elections to legitimize his takeover of the government and show the world he was in charge. His name was the only one on the ballot. By that time, I had been transferred to a small town south of Cairo. I was assigned to take charge of a voting station there. My instructions were simple: I was to tell the illiterate peasants to place their thumb print on the ballot and leave the rest of the ballot blank (because most of them could not write, their fingerprint was their signature). They were happy to do as instructed and leave quickly to tend to the fields. The instructions also directed me to fill every ballot with Nasser's name. I wasn't surprised when the government declared to the world that he had won 96% of the vote.

The World Bank's refusal to finance a dam project, infuriated

Nasser. The dam was needed to generate electricity to be used to create industries and allow farmers to plant a second crop during the yearly Nile floods. As a result, Nasser decided in 1956 to nationalize the Suez Canal to use its revenue to finance the project. The canal authority was a privately owned company belonging to investors mainly in England and France. The inevitable outcome was war with a coalition of British and French armies. Israel joined in to counter guerilla attacks from the Gaza Strip, which was occupied by Egypt at the time.

There were two other reasons for Israel's involvement. The first was the fact that Egyptian operatives had stopped most of the ships heading for Israel by preventing them from passing through the canal and confiscating their cargoes. The second was that Egypt controlled a choke point at Sharm El Sheik on the Red Sea Gulf of Aqaba, preventing an alternative route for its ships. During that war, the British conducted a raid on Cairo Airport, destroying many war planes on the ground. Nasser retaliated by sinking forty ships, belonging to several nations, in the canal, blocking it. French paratroopers conducted raids on the Egyptian garrisons in the area of the canal, and the British conducted the first helicopter attack in history there also. It was a time of extreme tension for the country.

During the outset of hostilities, Cairo Municipality employees were instructed to bring a blanket and report to a certain site on the outskirts of Cairo to receive weapons training to protect the fatherland. I did as I was requested to do so as not to seem unpatriotic, although I knew it was futile and that we were no match for Israeli and French paratroopers who might attack during the conflict. A handful of co-workers did likewise. When we arrived at the training site, we were each handed a British Lee Enfield rifle of WWI vintage and given instructions on how to fire it. We lay prone in the dirt and aimed at a half-inch steel plate placed against a dirt bank. The gun had a kick like a mule's and the bullets pierced the plate. I couldn't have imagined that a bullet could pierce such a thick plate. With this archaic weapon, we were supposed to fight battle-hardened paratroopers equipped with machine guns? Fortunately, the conflict ended before we were called upon to use those rifles. The canal stayed closed for almost a year, until all the sunken ships were removed.

Foreign exodus
Shortly after the war, Nasser gave notice to all foreigners and Jews to leave the country, stating that they were no longer welcome, in spite of the fact that Greeks and Italians had been in Egypt since Alexander the Great and the Roman conquest. He gave them a relatively short period of time to make their preparations before meeting the deadline to leave the country. Those entrusted with executing the order held onto the paperwork and did not notify the Jews until two days before the deadline. The short notice did not allow them to sell their businesses and their personal property at a reasonable price. Our apartment building housed several Jewish families who kept mostly to themselves. It was a traumatic experience for them reminiscent of the exodus. Their youth, however, looked forward to their move to Israel, danced the *"Hora"*, a Jewish folk dance, and sang *"Hava Nagila"* and other Hebrew songs at the top of their voices. It was a gutsy and foolhardy thing to do since tensions were high and they could be attacked by a mob.

Their elders worried and went through the tragic process of liquidating their belongings at fire-sale prices. One of them asked our family to come look at what they were forced to get rid of, in hopes of making a sale. We went to a neighbor's apartment and bought a sofa for the somewhat-low price they placed on it. The next morning, a Jewish friend of my nephew's who was being deported came to visit and urged him to look at the wall outside our apartment in order to show him that the Moslem Brotherhood had painted a cross beside the doors of every Christian family in the building. His ominous prediction was, "You are next."

Another outcome of the World Bank's refusal to finance Nasser's pet dam project was his decision to approach the Soviet Union to assist in the engineering and financing of the dam. Nikita Khrushchev received him in Moscow with open arms and signed an agreement to design and supervise the dam construction. Along with that endorsement, the Russian chairman pledged to help modernize the Egyptian armed forces, supplying them with heavy tanks, ammunition and MIG fighter planes. The Egyptian government paid for this hardware and the cost of the dam by exporting cotton and other agricultural products to Russia.

The inevitable outcome of this agreement was shortages of food, rationing and increased inflation. Life became harder, and my sister, her two sons and I found it difficult to survive on the dwindling value of my salary. We had to obtain coupons each month to buy the kerosene we used to fuel our cooking stove. Cooking oil and several other essential items were also rationed. My sister used creative ways to create meals. Some of her results didn't taste good at all, but we bit the bullet and swallowed them. Before Nasser speeches, the market was flooded with food imports and other rare commodities from the Soviet block to put the people in the right mood of mass euphoria upon hearing his speech. Those items disappeared right after the speeches. Also, due to the worsening relations with the West, especially the US, hard currency became unavailable.

Yet another war

In 1967, Nasser felt compelled to confront Israel. He thought that, with overwhelming numbers (1000 tanks and 100,000 infantry) it could be done. He coordinated a joint attack with the armies of Jordan and Syria and declared with great fanfare he intended to push Israel into the sea, then he started moving his forces into Sinai toward the border. The Israelis decided to take the initiative. Their air force made a pre-emptive strike which decimated the Egyptian air force in Cairo. With no air cover, the heavy hardware in the Sinai, which was purchased at great cost from Russia, was reduced to a vast junkyard in the desert. Officers discarded their uniforms, bought or swiped Bedouin dress and trickled back to Cairo. That conflict lasted only six days and resulted in the occupation of the Sinai by Israel, ruining the reputation of Egypt among its Arab neighbors. It also further worsened its economy, which had been in bad shape since Nasser had taken charge of the country.

Nasser was devastated by the defeat and gave a speech in which he offered his resignation. Huge crowds spontaneously took to the streets all over Cairo and with great emotion begged him not to step down. He had no choice but to remain as president. As a result of the losses incurred in the war, the economy neared total bankruptcy and Nasser declared that any government employee who wanted to leave the country was welcome to do so. I believed the economy had deteriorated to the point the government had to print money to pay employee salaries (the great majority of the population worked for the government). It was the beginning of the end for Nasser and his flirtation with socialism. He had a heart attack in 1971 and died shortly afterwards. While I hated the fact that my country was defeated and financially in bad shape, I found a glimmer of hope I may be able, at last, to emigrate and leave all the discrimination and unfair treatment I had endured during his rule.

Nasser's socialist government had made it illegal for government employees with a college education to resign and banned travel abroad except for those with medical emergencies whose treatment was unavailable in the country. That claim had to be attested to by ten doctors. Rumor had it that if any doctor signed such claim, he would either disappear or have his license to practice medicine yanked. The only other allowable reason to leave would be for those who were invited by a foreign company for business consultations, provided that all expenses would be borne by the foreign company. No one was allowed to do business abroad except people connected to the regime. Those restrictions were so draconian that they almost prevented my brother Naguib from pursuing his goal to emigrate. He had to be very creative to devise ways to get around the ban; more on that later.

During his seventeen years in power, Nasser's effect on the country had some positive aspects and some negative ones. His policies included involving the country in several wars and ruining the economy. His original goals were noble. He wanted to free the country from foreign influence, reduce oppression on the lower class and inspire them to be proud again. During his regime, the government finally took action against the Moslem Brotherhood terrorist group, arresting and jailing hundreds of its members, including Dr. Ayman el Zawahry (who eventually became the leader of Al Qaeda after the death of Osama Bin Laden). During their trial, it was revealed they had been tortured.

After Nasser's death, Anwar el Sadat took over as president, dismantled the Soviet-inspired socialism and ousted the Soviet advisers. He made a surprise attack on the Israelis occupying the Sinai Peninsula. President Carter brokered a truce and persuaded the two sides to reach an agreement to end the state of war between them. While Sadat achieved these great improvements for the country, he also sided with the Moslem Brotherhood and allowed discrimination against the Christians to worsen. He was assassinated by Moslem fanatics while reviewing an army parade. His assassination was probably carried out because he shook the hand of Israel's President, Menachem Begin, and signed the agreement ending the state of hostilities, accepting the status quo.

Chapter 3
MY FAMILY

Dad

My parents did not seem to have much in common during my childhood but they must have loved each other because they had nine children including me. They did have a unique relationship, my childish impressions notwithstanding. My father, Nashed Boss, was born around 1892 in Sohag, a southern city of Egypt. By the time I was born, he had retired from the position of Chief Clerk in one of the southern provinces, an influential and enviable job at the time, especially for a Christian. He attained that position because he was probably the only one who could read, write and do math in town. He was self-taught since "education" in that part of the country was confined to memorizing the Qur'an.

During the time I knew him, he always carried a cane but seldom used it to lean on. I suppose it was part of the image he liked to project. Every morning he donned his *Tarbush* or fez (a red, woolen, brimless hat with a tassel at the back) and walked to a small coffee shop where they served the usual tiny cups of very thick Turkish coffee that one almost chewed rather than drank. He liked to play backgammon there to pass the time.

Dad hated haggling over the price of merchandise although haggling was and still is standard procedure in Egypt. All street hawkers quoted a high price to start the bargaining process. I

Parents' wedding in 1907

remember on one occasion my father called down to a grape vendor and, after the man climbed the stairs to the fourth floor, my father asked him the price. When the guy quoted an outrageous amount, my father was so enraged he took the whole basket and tossed its contents on the landing, telling him he was a gouger and a thief. The guy never uttered a word, left everything on the landing and came back a short while later with a policeman. I was alarmed about what would happen next, but my father presented his business card which showed his position as a retired high-ranking government employee.

**Official photo of the administration where my dad
worked (he is seated in the middle)**

The policeman must have reasoned that if he did something
that might offend my father, his superior might punish him for
bothering a man who probably outranked the boss. The outcome
was predictable. The cop turned on the hawker and asked him,
"How dare you accuse this respectable gentleman?" He told him
to collect his grapes and hustled him down the stairs. I was
impressed by my father's influence but, at the same time,
embarrassed by his conduct. That kind of behavior was not
unusual in a society with such disparity between its classes.

On one occasion, Father declared that he had decided to discontinue paying our puny weekly allowance because we made a racket that woke him up during his afternoon nap. Mine was the equivalent of about a nickel, which I used to buy a small Japanese toy car or a piece of candy. Wilson, my eldest brother organized the first family rebellion against Father's hegemony. He handed each one a pot and told us to use a spoon, knife or fork to bang on it when he gave the signal, during fathers nap, to express our protest. This, of course, was an irresistible occasion for the rest of us to rebel and we participated with enthusiasm. An enraged Father emerged from his room ready to punish the culprit who dared to wake him up, but was surprised to see all of us. Mother persuaded him to restore our allowance to prevent a family rift. He never took that course again. Wilson was a born leader. Dad was never the same after that incident. He seemed to have lost all his enthusiasm for reforming us or participating in planning family activities.

Dad was not a religious man. One of his favorite quotes was, "The priests have hoodwinked us into believing." My mother, however, did take me to church occasionally. I attended Bible class and was handed glossy, colored pictures of Jesus and the saints, which impressed me. I did not like going to church, however, because the service lasted three hours. People would come in at different times and leave at any time. The priest would go down the aisles swinging an incense burner, which offended my nose and stung my eyes. He intoned incantations in an unintelligible language. (The Coptic language is remotely related to Ancient Egyptian, but written in Greek characters. Today the service is conducted in Arabic.) The hymns were chanted by male employees of the church who sounded like a bunch of crows, an altogether unpleasant experience.

My brother Naguib told me recently that my maternal grandmother, Farouza Abdel Malek, used to needle my father by calling him Nashed *Karakisha*, which meant Nashed Crunch. The reason: my grandfather, on his side of the family, worked as a boatswain (bos'un) of a cargo rowboat and gave his crew dried-out bread that crunched when they ate it. Father, in turn, called mother Helana *Nugr-el-teen* (to distinguish themselves from the Moslems, Copts often adopted western first names for females). The added epithet meant "borer in the mud" because her father had been a surveyor and his men would poke a measuring pole in the mud of land that had been newly created by Nile silt.

Mom after the birth of the first male child in 1917

They had a weird sense of humor.

Mother

Mom was twenty years younger than Dad. Her family was richer than his. Grandmother never let him forget that fact, and even claimed she was younger than he. Mothers-in-law can be challenging at times! Mom graduated from the American school in Asyut in the south of Egypt. She was a homemaker and a gentle, loving person who cooked wonderful, delicious food and supervised a servant who cleaned the house. She mended our clothes and showed us love. Most of the time, she was calm and not easily ruffled. Her first pregnancy ended in a miscarriage, the second child died at the age of one. All nine children (four girls and five boys) that followed survived.

One day, Mother missed some money she had set aside. She told Dad who asked the maid about it. The maid denied emphatically but there was no other explanation for the loss. Dad then told Ahmad, the doorkeeper (a sort of concierge) at our apartment building about his suspicion that the newly hired maid, must have stolen it. Ahmad was a decent and dignified individual despite his lowly position. He was always courteous to our family and sometimes ran errands for us. Ahmad said he would take care of it. He came to our apartment carrying a whip and asked the girl about the money. She denied like before, so he gave her a severe whipping that, to my young eyes, was extremely cruel. Finally after realizing that he would not cease until the truth came out, she stopped screaming, admitted that she took it and extracted it from her clothing. Of course she lost her job and was handed to the police.

In Egypt at that time such cruelty could happen without repercussion. Thievery was a hazardous calling. Whenever a thief was observed stealing, we heard the cry, *"Haramy,*

haramy" (thief, thief), and a race would start. A mob would form immediately and chase the guy until they caught him and beat him without mercy before handing him over to the cops. It was a great deterrent... inhumane, but effective.

Mom took the initiative when the time for summer vacation arrived. She and one of my older sisters would take the train to Alexandria to find a cabin or an apartment to rent, something that is usually handled by fathers. She knew if she left that task to Dad, we would never go anywhere. As mentioned above, Dad hated anything that had to do with negotiating (in this case, haggling over the rent) and deputized her to travel and make all arrangements. She then sent a letter telling us where to come and meet her (we had no telephone). She was very good at doing all that was necessary.

Members of the family in Alexandria
I am standing on the far left

She chose the best beach to go to and found where the food shops were and how far it was to the water, etc. Once we reached Alexandria, we became instant beach bums, spending all day in the sun and water. Our skin turned from tan to dark brown and started to peel off after a couple of weeks, making us look as if we had some awful skin disease. We enjoyed that time tremendously.

During that time mom prepared our lunch every day. On some days, it consisted of sliced potatoes in a large baking pan with chunks of beef and sliced roma tomatoes, onion, butter and spices on the top. We took the pan to a nearby baker who placed it alongside his bread in the oven and gave us a receipt. After we emerged from the sea around noon, we were famished and raced to the baker to claim the tray. It had the most delicious aroma and a taste to match. It was one of many memorable meals she prepared. Mom never punished us when we misbehaved. She just gave the culprit "the look" and that was enough to straighten him or her up. On rare occasions, when things really got out of hand, she told Dad and he administered the necessary discipline.

Alexandria's large contingent of Greeks and Italians made it more cosmopolitan and tolerant toward Christians than the more conservative Cairo. It also had cooling sea breezes and was a clean, beautiful city, free of the ever-present dust of Cairo. It is the second largest city in the nation and was founded by Alexander the Great, who created it in 331 B.C. by connecting an island to the mainland with a causeway. He also built Pharos, which was a combination library and lighthouse to guide ships. It was one of the seven wonders of antiquity. The library contained most of the original, one-of-a kind writings of Greek philosophers and other treasures that were lost when it burned to the ground. At least, that was the legend I heard when I was a child. Reading about it recently, I learned it was destroyed in an earthquake in the 14th century. Modern Alexandria has a 15 mile long shoreline that was a Mecca for both Egyptians and tourists because of its fine beaches. We enjoyed going there each summer to swim and ogle the bikini-clad girls (that mode of dress is no longer allowed except at beaches frequented by foreigners). It also had a good light-rail system which is still in operation today.

The summer I became six I had a bad surprise. Mom had rented a ground floor apartment in Alexandria for the summer. One morning I was in the bathroom and heard the rest of the family preparing to leave. I assumed they would wait for me and took my time. When I got out, I realized they had left. I did not want to spend the rest of the day cooped up while everyone was having fun. After the initial panic, I thought about going out through the front door to follow them but remembered that if I did, I would have to leave it unlocked (it was not self-locking), so I opened one of the windows, climbed out and jumped to the street below. The window sill was about five feet above street level. I reached up, pushed the shutters closed using my fingertips and went searching for them. I had no idea where they were heading but I struck out and was lucky to find them after five minutes of running. My mother was furious that nobody had noticed my absence, but she calmed down afterward. I guess she realized she hadn't noticed my absence either.

We move

When I reached the age of four, Mom got fed up with the cramped space in the apartment in which I was born. She took me with her as a chaperone and went looking for a larger apartment. First, she looked at a nice ground floor apartment which had a separate toilet in addition to a full bathroom. It also had parquet floors but only four rooms. There were, however, three strikes against it: The street noise and dust would have been excessive in that notoriously dusty city; the size was too small for our huge family, and it did not get any sun, which, she felt, would affect our health. The apartment she selected was less luxurious, had five rooms but only one bathroom with a single toilet and a small kitchen to serve all eleven of us. One room was used for reception and the rest became bedrooms. Access to the two farthest bedrooms was through the first one. A twelve-foot-wide hallway served as a dining and family room. The apartment was located on the top floor of a four-story apartment building away from the bustle of the street. The stairway was twice as large as our apartment. It was clad in Carrara marble from Italy with wrought iron guardrails and large landings providing access to four apartments each. We had to climb those labor-intensive stairs two or three times a day and became so experienced at it, we ran up or down two steps at a time. It was good exercise, I guess. I was disappointed when she settled on that second one and we moved there. Even at my young age, I could evaluate design and aesthetics; however, the other considerations that swayed Mother were just as important, if not more so.

At the end of the final semester in college, just before I started work on my thesis project, my mother, whose health had been deteriorating for some time, died. Her death was the worst tragedy that had befallen our family, and I cried bitterly at the loss. A year later, my grieving father died. My class attended both funerals and tried to console me. To drown my sorrows, I buried myself in the thesis project. The jury, which was composed of most of the architectural faculty, awarded it a good grade (juries did not allow the students to make a presentation to defend their effort). I came third in my graduating class in spite of a rumor that there was an unwritten law that the first three in a graduating class in any school had to be Moslem. I must have had good advocates on that jury, which included two Coptic professors. This outcome made no difference whatsoever in my career since talent and ability were not considered to be factors in placement or advancement in Egypt. What mattered was who your relatives were and what your religious background was. I had no Moslem relatives, refused to bribe anyone and belonged to the "wrong" religion.

Chapter 4
MY SIBLINGS

My Sisters

My four sisters were Charlotte, Hilda, Olga and Laura. Each had a distinct and unique personality. All are very dear to me and I miss them. Laura, the youngest, is the only surviving sister. She is 88 years old now and still resides in Egypt and, until 10 years ago, used to travels to the U.S. once a year to visit her daughter in North Carolina and her son in New Jersey. I will describe each according to their age, from the eldest to the youngest, highlighting how I related to them.

When I was about four or five years old, my eldest sister, Charlotte, needed my services as a chaperone for a trip to Grandma in Heliopolis, a Cairo suburb. Charlotte discovered at the last moment that all my clothes were dirty. It was a Sunday when my aunts, who lived with my grandma, baked devil's food and angel food cakes which were heavenly. I was eager to ride on the metro, go get my treats, and use the swing in the backyard, but when she told me I would have to dress in one of Laura's dresses, I refused in disgust. However, after considering the alternative, which was to miss all the cake and fun, I grudgingly agreed after she assured me that nobody would know the difference. I had a great time at Grandma's house, like I always did. Of course they were amused at my appearance.

When I was ten, Charlotte would take me as a chaperone to the movies since, in Egyptian society, women were not allowed to go places by themselves because most men would confer unwanted advances on them. Once she made the mistake of taking me to a film starring Fred Astaire and Ginger Rogers doing their dance numbers. I hated watching this genre with a passion since I wanted to see action movies. During a scene which happened to be particularly interesting to her, I whispered, "I want to go to the bathroom." She said, "Hold on a moment until this scene is finished." Since I was spoiled and bored senseless, I repeated my request a couple of times at short intervals and, when that did not produce immediate results, I shouted, "I WANT TO PEE!" All the people around us burst out laughing. This embarrassed her and she had to take me to the restroom. Boys can be a pain sometimes.

After waiting for a long time for Mr. Right to come along and ask for her hand, Charlotte married Michael, a math teacher whom she didn't care for, to avoid becoming an old maid of 28. He turned out to be a drunkard and we discovered later that he was a devil-worshiper dabbling in the occult. He made life miserable for her and their three daughters. One cannot imagine what torture he made them endure as evidenced by holes in the walls, broken doors and a miserable, terrorized wife and children. Charlotte developed rheumatoid arthritis and wasted away in front of our eyes and we could do nothing about it because Egyptian law gives the husband the right to do anything to his family short of killing them. She died of her illness a couple of years after I immigrated to the US. It was a family tragedy; she was only 62.

Hilda was in charge of bathing me in our largest cooking pot when I was a child. She used scalding hot water for that purpose. I think she believed that she had to peel my skin off to get rid of the thick layer of dirt she imagined was there. After enduring this ordeal a few times, I put my foot down and with folded arms refused to step in the pot. She tried to persuade me but I was adamant. Then she had an inspiration and said, "Suit yourself. If you don't get in, you will stay here naked, covered with suds until you turn wormy." That did the trick. I could picture worms crawling all over me and agreed to be boiled alive. Mary decided not to go to the university after finishing high school. She married Hanna, a nice guy who worked for BOAC (British Overseas Airways Corporation, now British Airways) and had two sons. One of them was Samir (Sam) whom I later sponsored for immigration to the U.S. He eventually formed a successful engineering company in Texas and became a tycoon.

Laura, like all my sisters, attended the *Lycée Français*, a top-rated high school with French teachers. She ultimately graduated from the university with a major in French literature. She was appointed as a French instructor at the university. Most of the Egyptian professors there could barely pronounce the language but gave her below-par evaluations. She was repeatedly bypassed for promotion because she is a Christian. She, on the other hand, could speak the language fluently. Her qualifications included spending a few months in Grenoble, France, for additional credits. Her career setbacks did not shock us because we knew that Christians were usually treated that way at that time. During a recent visit, I escorted her to the French club in our retirement community. She conversed with the native French members and even corrected the grammer for one of them. Their leader sent an e-mail to the members stating she spoke better French than they did!

Naguib introduced Laura to a fellow student while he was attending the University of Cairo. Waheeb was about ten years her senior and after they dated for a short period, he proposed and she accepted. She had two boys in quick succession. When she got pregnant again, my sister Olga, who sensed that

Wahib's family preferred boys, had the following conversation with him:

"Are you wishing for a boy or a girl?"
"I don't like to speculate about things that I can do nothing about."
"People usually have preferences. Suppose she gave birth to a girl, would you be happy?"
"Impossible, it is not in my nature to produce girls. Would you like to bet?"

In Egypt, boys are preferred over girls by some fathers because they don't have to worry about a daughter being molested by somebody or becoming an old maid. This can be a burden on the family. In spite of Waheeb's assertions, Laura did give birth to a daughter, Louisette and two years later she had Yvette. Her husband learned to love daughters after that. I used to tell their kids far-out stories that thrilled them and fired up their imaginations. They still remember that experience to this day. They are happily married now and their children are married also. How time flies!

At the age of 49, after Laura gave birth to Yvette, Waheeb became sick. The doctors could not pinpoint what was wrong, other than to say it was a virus, a catchall word at the time. He died shortly after, leaving her to raise the four children by herself. Because he was well-to-do, Linda was well provided for. She was also left with all the headaches associated with keeping that wealth, including a lawsuit from one of Waheeb's brothers, a lawyer, who wanted Waheeb's share to revert back to the family to increase his share of the inheritance. In addition, there were claims by squatters in an apartment building Laura and Waheeb owned in Alexandria. This resulted in drawn-out court proceedings. She dealt with all that in addition to raising the children and teaching at the university. She is a remarkable woman.

Laura's youngest son, Sidhom, took longer than usual to graduate from the university and had to repeat failed classes. Finally, he graduated as a civil engineer and immigrated to the U.S. where he suffered tremendously from loneliness. When he visited us in Massachusetts, he described the girl he would marry as being a quiet sort who would obey his every word, abide by all his decisions and stay at home. After failing to find such a mythical person stateside, he went back to Cairo and his family arranged for him to meet Nashwa. After a very short engagement, they got married and returned to the States. Nashwa turned out to be smart and feisty, which forced Sidhom to change his chauvinistic ways. She passed the engineering licensing exam the day after she returned to New Jersey from attending her grandmother's funeral in Egypt. The first time we met her we were surprised because she had turned Sidhom's attitude completely around. We were amused to see him doing things we would never have guessed he would do. They now have two girls, own their own home as well as a vacation house, are active in their church and continue to live the American dream.

My brothers

I had four brothers: Wilson, the eldest, was born after Charlotte (father named him Wilson after President Woodrow Wilson). He was the only male in our family with a western name. He was followed by Naguib, Amin, Sobhi, Laura and me. Naguib, Sobhi, Laura and I are the only survivors today. Since I had more dealings with my brothers than my sisters, I have allocated more space to describe my dealings with each.

Wilson had a strong character but a tendency to keep people at arm's length. He would rather be feared and respected than loved. He held his own in school despite taunts from his schoolmates stemming from his "foreign" name. In high school, Wilson joined the field hockey team and learned to play the game. One weekend, he decided to form a family team and designated old broom handles as hockey sticks. The girls fashioned torn stockings into a ball of sorts. The flat roof of our apartment building was our field and we played that game with enthusiasm. Wilson stopped fights with a frown and a few choice words. Nobody dared upset him lest he or she be subjected to what one perceived to be an unimaginable wrath or possibly corporal punishment. Whether that was true, nobody dared find out.

Once, we discovered a mouse in the apartment and the chase was on. Everybody took a swat at it until one well placed whack finished it. I took a shoe and hit it after it was good and dead. Wilson thought that was admirable because it showed guts for a four-year-old. He rewarded me with a small coin, which made me very happy and proud of my "accomplishment." He tried to browbeat Naguib, who was two years younger than he, once too often. Naguib confronted him and told him that if he ever spoke to him in that manner again, he would kill him. Wilson realized that he had stepped over the line and never bothered him after that. Naguib was more robust than Wilson but had a sunny disposition.

Wilson was an avid reader who often went to used book stores and bought British novels. Of course, when he finished one, Naguib read it and on down the line until it came to me. I started reading them with the aid of a dictionary. The books were extremely interesting and it was difficult to stop at the end of each chapter. I remember reading about the adventures of Captain Horatio Hornblower of the British Navy. It was full of discouraging terms like names of the masts and sails and the ranks of the crew. Words like "mizzen mast" and "t'gallant" (top gallant) sails and "bos'n" (boat-swain) as well as many other nautical terms. It was touch and go and I was forced to use the dictionary all the time but I persevered and enjoyed it tremendously. Eventually, I got the hang of the language and could hazard guesses as to what the words I didn't know meant. Another interesting novel was the 500+page *Beau Sabreur* by P. C. Wren. It was about the French Foreign Legion in Morocco. I still remember passages from it to this day. When I was dating my future wife, Gayle, I told her how interesting it was. She borrowed it from the library and read the whole thing in a few sittings and told me how much she enjoyed it too.

Wilson went on to become a pharmacist. After working several years for the Egyptian government and later at a private pharmaceutical lab, he developed a toothpaste that became popular during WWII when imports were stopped. Being intelligent and seeing that the future for Copts in Egypt was bleak and being cognizant of the fact that professionals had a much better chance to move ahead in the world abroad, he decided to try his luck exploring his chances there. I suspect that all his hard work prior to making that decision was to save enough to start life in the US. His decision to emigrate was made during King Farouk's reign, when no restrictions were imposed on travel or transferring money abroad.

It was around the time when the Moslem Brotherhood uprising occurred that Wilson decided there was no future for him in a country that offered limited opportunities for any Christian (or Moslem for that matter, since the country had no drug-manufacturing plants). Having reached the height of excellence in his profession, he needed room to grow. He must have also sensed that the country was heading for rough times and

Ezzat, Hilda and Olga

**Olga, Laura and some of their daughters
in front of the king's palace in Alexandria**

decided to devise a plan to realize his dream. To achieve it, he applied for a scholarship based on his experience and excellent academic record and was accepted at Purdue University in Lafayette, Indiana. Based on this, he received a visa from the US Embassy and bought a ticket on a cargo ship that had cabins for a few passengers.

Wilson then traveled to Alexandria to spend the night before boarding the ship the following morning. He tried to find a room in a hotel but the few hotels that existed at the time were all booked. Not wanting to spend a miserable night at the terminal, he pretended to be a foreigner since foreigners were accorded special consideration and granted rooms that were kept in reserve for such an eventuality. He had a darker complexion than the rest of us which went well with his pretended nationality. He affected a Pakistani accent and told the receptionist, "I come from Pakistan and would like to get a room for one night." That did the trick and he went to the port the next morning refreshed and ready to meet the challenge of starting a new life in the States.

He worked as an usher during ball games to help support himself. While at Purdue, he met Ruth, a post-graduate student whom he dated and later married. He earned a PhD, had a son and occupied an influential position at Johnson & Johnson Pharmaceutical Corporation. Among his responsibilities was the task of securing approvals from the FDA for new products introduced by the company. His success inspired his younger brother Naguib to follow suit a few years later. Twenty years after he immigrated, I asked Wilson to sponsor me for immigration to the US. It is thanks to him and his wife that I was able to do so. Wilson died in 1990 from acute liver failure.

Naguib, the next in line, is my favorite brother. He is an

extrovert with an upbeat personality and a cheerful demeanor. He used to gather Sobhi, Laura and me when we were little and interpret English novels he inherited from Wilson. He'd recount them in his inimitable, interesting and dramatic way, holding us in thrall. He read one chapter during each session. We always begged him to continue, but each novel was 400 or 500 pages long and we had to wait to find out what happened in the next chapter. It was like a serialized TV show (TV hadn't been invented then). These episodes were the highlight of our day. Naguib also organized us into a ping-pong team. After meals, we would clear the table and install a homemade net to play for an hour or so of great competitive fun. I became quite skilled at it and later used that skill when I played the real game after joining the YMCA in Cairo. I had a mean left-hand shot that was almost impossible to return.

Naguib graduated from the College of Agriculture at Cairo University. When he couldn't find a job in his field, he found one as a surveyor for the British army stationed in Cairo since he had studied surveying in college. The job didn't pay much but it was a living. He used to tell us stories about his work, and I remember one where he told us about a co-worker, an Iraqi filing clerk, who said, "I am sick and tired of having to look for files. I wish they would invent a system that would allow me to call out, 'File number 368' and it would reply in a small voice, 'Here I am.' His wish must have been prophetic since it preceded the invention of the computer!

After that job came to an end, Naguib applied for a position at the Egyptian Railways Department in response to an ad in the paper calling for experts in agriculture. He became excited at the prospect of working in his field. After he was hired, he discovered that the job required him to travel long distances by train in response to reports from the switchmen stating a tree has fallen due to "the winds." After inspecting a few of these "wind" stories, he discovered switchmen had actually cut the tree to light fires to keep warm in winter! Since each tree had to be accounted for, they telegraphed to authenticate it had died of natural causes. Finally, the constant travel and futility of the job got to him, so he resigned to try his hand at being an entrepreneur.

To pursue that goal, he obtained a license to export Egyptian henna, a product desirable to the cosmetics industry in the States. He was thwarted at every step by Moslem regulators who wanted exorbitant bribes to grant him an export permit and by sellers who would add cheap foreign substances to the product. He also tried exporting beeswax and, after he won the bid, the government permitting authority decided to award the contract to a Moslem who had placed a higher bid. The "winner" offered him a lower price for the wax Naguib had already bought and, since he was stuck with the lot and had no way of moving it, he agreed. The buyer brought an unassuming, shabbily dressed individual to inspect the shipment. He turned out to be an expert who chose some wax discs and rejected others. When Naguib asked why, the guy sawed through one of the rejected discs and showed him that the core was stuffed with dirt!

When he found out the cards were stacked against him, Naguib decided to emigrate in spite of all the obstacles placed on travel by the Nasser regime. He decided to challenge the odds and went to the Canadian embassy to apply for immigration because he thought that Canadians were more tolerant of minorities than Americans. A few days later, he received a rejection so he wrote a note to the Minister of Immigration in Canada thanking him for preventing him from making a grave mistake by choosing Canada instead of the US. He mentioned he should have chosen the US since he had a brother there who would be glad to sponsor him. A few days later, he received a letter from the Canadian embassy inviting him to come. When he went, the receptionist told him he was the first Egyptian to be approved for immigration to Canada and asked, "What did you do?" When he said he browbeat the top guy and forced him to acquiesce, she laughed. His passport was stamped with an entry visa to Canada. The first obstacle was overcome by his sheer tenacity. He then wrote to McGill University in Canada applying to study animal husbandry. A couple of weeks later, he received a letter informing him that the course wasn't offered there but he could apply at Rutgers University in New Jersey which accepted one student every two years. He decided to deal with this issue when he arrived in Canada.

His next obstacle was to get an exit visa from the Egyptian government. Since he was doing business with the Eastern Block, he was eligible to apply for an exit visa to travel abroad to negotiate an agreement for export. Naguib asked a friend of his who had dealings with a pump manufacturer in Czechoslovakia to contact them and ask that they invite him by name to discuss a deal. A few days later, he received a telegram inviting him personally to Czechoslovakia and stating that the manufacturer would bear all expenses. He thought this would allow him to get the visa but, when he went to the Cairo exit visa office, the employee looked at his distinctively Christian name and the document then said that a telegram is not considered a legal document and he must get a stamped letter from the Czechoslovak Consul.

Naguib bit the bullet, went to the consulate and asked to see the consul. He smiled at the secretary and told her his story in his charming way. She said, "No problem," wrote the letter, placed a huge official stamp on it and got the consul, who was on the phone at the time, to sign it. He did so without reading it. The letter stated that the discussion was urgent and must be done with Naguib personally. With that document in hand, he went to the visa office, thinking that he had complied with all requirements. The employee read it and, with a look of astonishment, he started following conversation:

Employee: "How in Hades did you get this letter?"
Naguib who hadn't read the letter: "What do you mean?"
Employee: "Have you read it?"

Naguib read it and was amazed to find that the secretary had written if Naguib was not allowed to leave for the meeting, the relations between Czechoslovakia and Egypt may be in jeopardy! Naguib hid his astonishment and replied:

"Yes, I have read it. Is the stamp large enough for you? Can I get my visa now?"
"I have never seen a stamp that size before; however, the papers must be sent to the secret police to make sure you are not wanted for any crimes against the government."

When Naguib asked him when he expected a reply, he told him: "Are you crazy? I hope nobody heard you. Nobody dares ask that question. They can keep it forever if they want to."

Hearing that final statement, Naguib realized that, after all the effort he had made, the letter had met a dead-end, so, he decided to risk all, went home and wrote his last will and testament then wrote a letter to President Nasser himself, something that nobody dares to do. A few days later, he received a letter bearing the secret police emblem and thought it would summon him for interrogation. To his relief, it contained instructions directing him to go to the exit visa office to receive his visa, provided he arrive at a certain time; otherwise, his application would be refused. When he checked his watch, he discovered he had only twenty minutes to make the trip to the government office, take the elevator to reach the fifth floor, and run to the office to present that letter to the bureaucrat.

He scrambled down the stairs two at a time, hailed a taxi and told the driver he would pay him two pounds over the meter fare if he made the trip in ten minutes. The driver drove through two red lights and arrived in nine minutes flat. The bureaucrat was surprised to see the letter and had to stamp the passport. That was a day of jubilation for Naguib. He booked a passage on a ship from Alexandria to Genoa, Italy, destined for Le Havre, France, where he would board a ship to Canada. Amin, another brother, decided to accompany him to help him and bid him adieu. When Naguib went to board the ship, the secret police agent told him to fill out a form. He erroneously cited the destination as Canada instead of Czechoslovakia. Amin stepped on his foot to alert him to his mistake. Naguib immediately realized what he had done, asked for another form and corrected that mistake, which could have canceled all his Herculean efforts to that point.

The police agent reviewed the answers and leafed through his passport and said, "Aha, I see you have a stamp from the French embassy to land in Le Havre. Can you explain that?" Naguib told him Czechoslovakia was a land-locked country and, since he was going by ship, he had to land in France to board a train to Prague. The agent said, "I know what you are going to do. You are not going to Czechoslovakia; you plan to go directly to Paris to have fun." Naguib said, "Yeah right! It will be easy to do so using my measly fifty pounds which the government allowed me to take." The agent saw that Naguib was not rattled and allowed him to board the ship. That guy missed noticing that the passport had a stamp allowing Naguib to enter Canada. We rejoiced for him but missed him terribly. In preparation for writing this memoir, I asked him for the details of his departure and he told me he learned on board ship that the Suez War had started and all travel outside the country had been stopped just hours after he left the country. He said he was elated he was able to leave Egypt before the borders were closed. It was another example of God's intervention on behalf of members of our family.

Before he left Egypt, Naguib had been accepted at Rutgers University in New Jersey for post-graduate studies in animal husbandry, a branch of genetics. When he arrived at Marseilles, Naguib took the train to Paris. On the train, he met Ingborg Bartmann, a German lady who worked as a language instructor at the Berlitz School in Paris. They enjoyed dating during his brief stay in France. After traveling to LeHavre, Naguib boarded a cruise ship to Canada. On arriving in Toronto, he corresponded with Rutgers to get information about starting his study there. He was informed there would be a one-month delay since his slot had been given to an Irish student who decided not to attend the course due to a death in the family and it would take that long to do the paperwork. They informed him of the date and address to which he should come.

The hostel where he stayed was occupied by two opposing factions of Irishmen. One was Protestant and the other Catholic. A member of one of the factions asked Naguib about his nationality, and when he found out he was from Egypt, he said, "Oh good, we can use you in our fight against the lousy Protestants." Naguib informed him he was not interested in participating in any war and went to the manager and explained that he did not want to share a room with members of either faction. She told him she would place him in a room currently occupied by a single Scotsman. To cut a long story short, that guy robbed him of his remaining $100. Naguib had to look for work in Canada to sustain himself during his wait and found a job as an assistant surveyor. At the appointed time, his admission to Rutgers arrived and he went to New Jersey.

During his sojourn in New Jersey, he continued to correspond with Ingborg and finally sent her a letter proposing marriage and inviting her to come to the US. She accepted and after a couple of weeks, she showed up at his doorstep. They had a ceremony attended by a few of his classmates. In due course, he received his master's degree in genetics. Eventually, they had two boys in quick succession then a daughter. Unfortunately, Ingborg could not bear to be away from Germany and they moved there. He had to learn German and find work in a country that was still influenced by Nazi intolerance of foreigners. When finally I was able to immigrate to the US, I traveled to Strassbourg from Paris by train to meet him and his family.

Naguib in Strasbourg, France

After applying for positions at several companies, he was accepted for employment as a researcher at Max Plank Institute, one of the premier research labs in Europe. He soon found that unless one had a PhD, he or she was considered a pawn to be ordered about and dismissed at the slightest infraction. You had to be addressed as *"Herr Doktor"* to earn any respect or occupy a meaningful position. He decided to work toward a PhD in genetics, and Ingborg helped him with the language. He succeeded in getting his doctorate and did important work at Max Plank. The company sent him to make presentations at symposia in New York and London. Now 94, he is retired and still lives in southern Germany. It seems that all of us who left the country—Wilson, Naguib and I— had great success and good advancements in our careers, which would have never occurred had we stayed in Egypt.

Both Amin and Sobhi worked as English teachers in Christian parochial schools. They remained in Egypt and had less adventurous lives compared to Wison and Naguib. Amin was my nemesis, whenever I said something that offended him, he would get mad and chase me. He could not catch me, however, because I would run around the dining table faster than he. This aggravated him and with a look of utter rage, he would stop and say " you will be punished". I knew then that it was futile to spend the whole day running around and getting him more pissed, so, I gave in and got thrashed. Of course, if Naguib was around, I would call his name and he would prevent him from doing so. Amin graduated from high school and went on to study English literature and drama at Cairo University. In his senior year, his professor arranged for his class to perform Shakespeare's *Macbeth* at the National Opera House. Amin gave us free tickets. While I didn't care for opera or Shakespeare and was not keen on watching Amin, I went just to see what the opera house looked like. I remember watching the three witches chanting over the cauldron and suddenly Amin jumped into the scene in his elaborate costume, shouting his one-liner, "Macbeth! Macbeth! Macbeth! Beware of MacDuff!" I almost laughed out loud but restrained myself.

Amin, the author, and nieces
Hilda is sitting at the right

Amin married my cousin Sisa (it is common for first cousins to marry in Egypt). He died at the age of 69 after being hit by a car driven by a wealthy Moslem woman who owned a factory. She bribed the sole witness who recanted the detailed testimony he had given to the police directly after the accident, and no charges were filed against her.

I relate to my brother Sobhi the most. He is personable and has a good sense of humor. He is five years older than I and used to tell me about his attempts to date girls. He even memorized a few words in Armenian and tried to engage a neighboring Armenian girl in conversation using the words. All I remember was a phrase he kept practicing; it sounded like *"Hosyagor pummosem"* which he said meant "Come here." Another phrase I remember was *"Egoor bededing amekneesa."* At least that was how he pronounced it. It was supposed to mean "Let's go for a walk." He never told me what the outcome was. When we were in Alexandria during my teens, we used to rent crude surfboards made of canvas stretched over a wooden frame and treated with some sort of white waterproof paint. Sobhi and I used to race them and tried to impress the girls with our derring-do.

When my family moved to the south of Egypt during WWII to escape the air raids, I accompanied Sobhi and went fishing in a pond no bigger than a backyard swimming pool. We each had a reed with a string ending with a hook which we baited with an earthworm we dug up. After waiting for about half an hour during which I watched the home-made float (a piece of cork) bob mildly from time to time, the line was tugged suddenly by a powerful creature that almost pulled my small frame into the water. I yanked the reed and pulled up a "huge" fish about the size of a grown man's palm. I couldn't believe a fish that size could come from such a small pond. My brother pulled a slightly smaller one a couple of minutes later. We ran home extremely excited, and mother cleaned and fixed them for our dinner. It was absolutely the tastiest fish I ever ate.

On another occasion, we went with a friend of his to a vacant lot to fly a kite we had fashioned from wax paper stretched over a bamboo frame. How exciting to see it soar in the sky! One day, Laura found detailed instructions in a French-language children's magazine on how to build a car using a matchbox, rubber bands and a propeller. We built that thing two or three times and all it did was shake and stay put. After the third try, we tore up that magazine to express our frustration.

Sobhi followed Amin's example after graduating from the Faculty of Liberal Arts (schools at the university were called faculties) and became an English teacher in a parochial school after graduating from college. He was popular with the students and many flocked to him for tutoring. This supplemented his salary and allowed him to buy items he would not have been able to purchase if he depended solely on his pay. He went to visit a friend and was introduced to his sister, Renee. She was pretty and had green eyes, which are rare in that part of the world. A few days later he met her by chance in the street and struck a conversation, something that is normally frowned upon in that society. They liked each other and he proposed and was accepted.

After a courtship of four months (chaperoned, of course), they got married and had two daughters. He is still living with his wife in a walk-up apartment on the fourth floor with a lot of stairs to climb, making it especially hard now that he is 90. We still correspond through e-mail. One of his daughters, Maha, later immigrated to the U.S. and lives with her family in California.

**Sobhi, Renee and their daughters,
Manal & Maha**

Chapter 5
MY EARLY YEARS AND EDUCATION

The early years

I was born in Cairo, Egypt. Like all my siblings, I was born at home. A midwife named Rachel assisted in the delivery. I discovered her name when I looked at my birth certificate much later. My birth was not planned. I was told later it was an unexpected surprise to my parents since my mother was 40 and my father was 60! My version is that they tried to produce a perfect specimen by experimenting with the eight births that preceded me and when I was born, "Voilà!" I was their masterpiece.

Since I was her last child, my mother spoiled me and let me sleep in her bed until I reached the age of eight. She endured my bed-wetting for much of that time. We had no space for an extra bed in the crowded apartment. A tradesman specializing in refurbishing cotton mattresses would come periodically to remove and discard the casing. He fluffed the cotton using a gizmo that looked like a one-stringed harp which he held on top of the cotton and banged on it with a large wooden mallet. He then placed the cotton in new material which he sewed closed. This made the mattresses as good as new and miraculously removed any lingering smell.

My sister Laura, who was three years older than I, liked to play "pretend". One very hot summer day when I was about five, she said, "Let's pretend that it's snowing". She dressed me in a fake fur coat she had and held an umbrella and started jumping up and down with glee while I sweated and felt I was about to die from the heat. This went on for about twenty minutes until I said I didn't want to play that game anymore. When I reminded her of that episode recently, she said she was extremely jealous of me when we were children because I had become the favorite of our mother, and all her friends fawned over me and said how cute I was. Now that I think about it, I recall her girlfriends would gather around me and make a fuss about my blondish curly ringlets and the dimples on my chubby hands. I hated that and I hated their feminine smell and fretted about the attention I got. My older brothers used to say, "You will regret that (being annoyed) when you grow up!" I had no idea what they meant.

At about the same age of five, my mother bought a small duck and let it loose in our apartment. It was a beautiful white bird and we got accustomed to its playful nature. It would peck at our legs whenever we passed by. It became a pet and we liked to feed it and chase it around. I had no idea that it was being fattened in preparation for being served for dinner. Finally, doomsday arrived, and mother cornered it and took it to the kitchen. I pleaded with all my heart and soul for sparing it and it pained mother to listen to my entreaties, but the inevitable happened. It was the first real tragedy in my life and I wept bitterly for the murder of "my friend". At dinner, I refused to partake in the wanton cannibalism in spite of taunting from my heartless siblings.

In a large family, the youngest is usually the one that insecure siblings pick upon and try to brow-beat to build their character. I became the target of this practice from two of my siblings who affected the shaping of my character in a negative way. During our childhood Laura, like Lucy in the *Peanuts* cartoon strip, took it upon herself to "set me straight". She never missed a chance to prove that anything I did was wrong. Whenever she criticized me, Sobhi, the brother who was close to her age would say, "Exactly!" with assured finality, agreeing with her. Based on this irrefutable testimony, I believed them and reached the erroneous conclusion that I was destined to roam the earth doing wrong things for the rest of my life! I became so convinced that Laura was always right, I did not resent her continuous ribbing or doubt her mostly erroneous judgments.

One day, the three of us went to a movie starring David Niven in the role of Rollo who was being harassed by his sister Celina in a manner similar to what Linda was doing to me. When we left the theater, I pointed at Lara and said "Celina" and to Sobhi and said "Rollo". They laughed sheepishly and stopped criticizing me from then on. My brother also stopped siding with her and life became easier. Who said that movies are a waste of time?

The other sibling who had an adverse effect on me was my brother Amin, who was seven years older than I and had misaligned eyes. This condition was caused by an accident when he was a baby. It affected his whole character. I suspect the kids made him miserable in school. He had a very limited sense of humor and would not tolerate any joshing from me. I, on the other hand, was too young to realize what I said at times angered or annoyed him. When that happened, he would get mad and chase me. I would run to the dining table and we would race round and round, first one way then the other. When he couldn't catch me, he would stop and get an ominous, enraged look on his face and say, between clenched teeth, "It is imperative that I hit you". I knew then that he meant business and that, even if we ran around the table all day, he would they became blunt so often. I never told her I was the culprit. This hobby helped me to devise ways to solve difficult problems. It took a lot of time and effort to finish one of those models and I had a great feeling of accomplishment when I finished them.

One day, Father, who had a short temper, became mad at me for something I did or didn't do. To punish me, he took my just-finished B-17 model and tossed it out of the window. It made its maiden and final flight all the way to the street four floors below. It made me so mad, I didn't say a word and I never forgave him for it. Building model aircraft became useful later on because it enabled me to understand how to draw plans and elevations and helped me to think in 3-D. This training made it easy for me to choose architecture, which requires imagination and disciplined thinking, as my future career.

My brother Sobhi told me recently that dad was a caring man who looked after the welfare of all my siblings and checked to make sure they were doing their homework. He answered their questions and explained things to them when they became stumped by a math problem or something that was difficult to understand. By the time I was born, however, he had reached the mandatory retirement age of 60. Idleness and possibly the constant problems of his nine children drove him to drink. He did not interact with me very much and became verbally abusive to mother. As a boy of four whose vocabulary wasn't extensive, I listened to the way he addressed her during his frequent tirades and it left no doubt in my young brain that he was saying bad words. I always objected when I heard his tone of voice when he was blaming her for something which he objected to. On one occasion, he used that same tone to ask her something and ended the sentence with, "*Ya sett el dar*". It sounded real bad to me so, I tried to object vehemently. However, I was surprised when they both laughed and thought become even angrier and get me in the end. So, I gave up and let him hit me to his heart's content. If Naguib, who was two years older than he, was at home, I would shout his name and he would come and sternly tell Amin to stop and he would grudgingly comply. I considered Naguib to be my hero. When I recounted this to my sister recently, she said she had the same experience and Naguib rescued her also.

Those beatings got so bad that one day, after Amin vented his wrath on me a little more than usual, I decided to leave home. I got dressed, left the house and started walking away. During my walk, I started visualizing how my absence would affect my mother and the anxiety that would result from my action and hoped that they would reach the conclusion that it was all Amin's fault. I walked for about a mile then I started thinking, *what will I eat without any money in my pocket to buy food? Where will I sleep?* When I realized I had no answers to these questions, I made a U-turn and headed back home. I was a thinking child.

During my early teens, I developed a passion for making model aircraft from scratch, using folder paper and tape (the lick-and-stick type). I borrowed American aircraft magazines from the library at the US embassy. Based on the pictures, I drew plans and elevations of the plane I intended to make a model for. Based on these drawings, I made a model of a B-17 and a B-25 bombers. I devised ways to fashion challenging parts of the fuselage. For example, I used discarded glass ampules (used when a doctor gave one of us an injection) to form the gun turrets. I formed engine cowlings by cutting lead wire-cladding in half and forming it around a dowel. I also experimented with propellers until I was able to make them turn by blowing on them. I cut them from tin cans using my mother's scissors, causing them to eventually become blunt. She wondered why that it was rather funny. My mother explained that *"Ya sett el dar"* meant "Oh, mistress of the house!"

My schooling

When I reached the age of seven, I attended *Madrasset al Zaher al Ebteda'iah* Primary School. (In Arabic, *madrasset* means school of, a form of *madrassah,* which means school, contrary to today's connotation of being a terrorist training institution for the Taliban. The *madrassah* was housed in a solidly built, castle-like building, had a dirt yard and a pocket-sized flower garden. The only sports we participated in were morning calisthenics. The school had classes in "horticulture". This meant that the teacher told us the Arabic names for flowers and pointed out what weeds looked like and then instructed us to pull those weeds. We were cheap labor and we learned nothing from that experience.

We also had music class. During the first class that I attended, I was full of anticipation about learning how to play a musical instrument. I was disappointed when the teacher distributed drums, horns and violins and I was given a stainless steel triangle and a rod. This was the last instrument left over because nobody wanted it. I had no idea what it was for and asked what I was supposed to do with it and how I was to play it. He said it was easy; all I had to do was bang away, so much for learning how to play music. Of course, being seven years old, I banged away with gusto and produced a racket. I do hope that the quality of teaching has improved since that time in 1937.

The first time I experienced overt discrimination occurred during my first year in school. I was seven at the time. One day, an announcement came over the public address system that the school was forming a scout troop and described the activity in glowing terms. I became excited at the prospect of participating in this new experience. The next day during recess, a teacher gathered the students around him in the school yard and started selecting those who would participate. He asked each student to state his name. When my turn came, he gruffly said, "No, not you" and selected the next boy. No reason was mentioned or possible participation in the future expressed. I was devastated and reached the erroneous conclusion that, for some reason, I was inferior and unworthy of joining. I had no idea Moslems discriminated against Christians, that Christian names are easily identifiable and that the basis for his action must have been my religion since he had never met me before. Much later, when I came face to face with the realities of life, I concluded this must have been the real cause for rejection.

The following week, while attending an English language class, a British inspector from the Department of Education visited our class (the British who established the education system in Egypt were still in charge of some departments in the ministry of education). He must have noticed my English pronunciation was better than the rest of the students. This prompted him to award me a novel about, of all things, the adventures of Hiawatha, the American Indian. I was delighted at the unexpected honor. Apparently, the Egyptian teacher, who had converted from Christianity to Islam was so dismayed at my receiving the book, he included my name in a list of students to be punished by the headmaster (Christians who converted to Islam, while rare, usually became the most fanatical and discriminating against their former fellow believers). All of those slated for punishment did not attend Moslem religion classes! He did not tell me he was sending me to be punished or that I had done something wrong (which I clearly hadn't since Christians were not required to attend Moslem prayers) or anything to give me a heads-up about what to anticipate.

My name was called on the public address system instructing me to proceed to the school yard where a group of older students were lining up. I had no idea what I was called for and thought it was some new and interesting activity. That group didn't seem to be in a good mood, however, and I soon learned why. The student at the head of that long line was being punished by the headmaster. School punishment in those days was a kind of torture consisting of severe caning with a supple 4-foot-long cane (made from an osier - a supple willow twig - about 3/8" in diameter). It was applied with force to the palm of the hand two or more time, depending on the severity of the offence. Being absent from Moslem prayer rated three strikes. I waited my turn not knowing why I was included in that group. If it was because of something I had done in the class from which I was summoned, it would have been odd; after all, my grades in English were among the best in the class and I had just been awarded a book by the inspector.

Anticipating punishment is usually worse than the actual act, especially if you are watching the cruelty inflicted upon student after student and the aftermath of each beating. My turn finally came and I neared the grim and forbidding demeanor of the ugly, stone-faced headmaster wielding his cane. The student ahead of me lost his nerve and withdrew his hand just as the last strike descended at warp speed making a whistling sound. It hit my leg and I sensed the impact but didn't feel a thing because it was so unexpected. After the headmaster delivered the prescribed punishment plus an extra one as retribution to the boy for withdrawing his hand, my turn came. I closed my eyes, extended my palm and winced at the thought of the excruciating pain I was about to receive. Stone-face tapped me on the shoulder and told me to move on. I suppose he thought he had imposed enough damage on such a young boy after he saw the welt forming on my leg, although I doubt he was capable of compassion. I felt hugely relieved and elated at my good fortune, even after my leg started to sting and turn red and blue.

When I returned home at the end of the school day, Mother noticed the mark on my leg right away and asked me about it. When I told her what had happened, a look of determination came over her face but she didn't say a word. Next day, I was surprised when she got dressed early and accompanied me to school, took me directly to the headmaster's office and told him in no uncertain fashion what she thought about what he had done. She was a woman of uncommon courage. It must have been a great surprise to Stone-face because, in that culture, women never confronted men in a situation like this (unfortunately, my father, who was 67 at the time, had stopped getting involved in our day-to-day affairs). Stone-face never changed expression or uttered a word.

Although all my brothers had attended that school, Mother took me out that day and enrolled me in a parochial school she had selected before she left home. It included both primary and secondary education but was in a shabby building. It was also much farther and did not serve the delicious free lunch the government school did. I remember watching the cook at the government school clean the tinned brass pots in the school yard; they were approximately five feet in diameter. I have no idea how he figured the amounts when he cooked the rice and other vegetables and meats. Now mother had to prepare my lunch which I carried in a stacked container and I walked about a mile to get to the new school. Life is unpredictable; it throws you surprises you have no control over.

Teachers at the new school were friendlier with the exception of Ahmad Qotb, who taught Arabic. All teachers of the Arabic language were mandated by the government to be Moslem since advanced Arabic language instruction was conducted in a Moslem-only *madrassah* which specialized in language and Qur'an instruction, where Christians were not allowed. He was the only teacher who utilized corporal punishment in that school. During the eight years I was a student there, I was caned every single class given by that monster. However hard I memorized the passage from the Qur'an (the holy Moslem book that we Copts were forced to recall verbatim), I blurted the first sentence and met his gimlet eye which showed he was just waiting for me to make a mistake, and froze. I knew if I missed a single word or mispronounced a syllable, I would be thrashed. A look of grim satisfaction came across his face at the prospect of indulging in his favorite pastime whenever I failed to continue.

After passing the nationwide high school graduation test, I applied to the School of Architecture, a branch of the School of Fine Arts in Cairo. A week later I received a letter informing me I had been accepted. I chose this school instead of the Department of Architecture at the School of Engineering at Cairo University after I found out the former was sponsored by a prince of the royal family, a patron of the arts who mandated that no tuition would be required and all drafting materials would be provided free by the school. While we were not poor and could afford to pay tuition at Cairo University, asking my father for money was like extracting teeth. I remembered watching my sister Laura beg for school fees and bus fare on several occasions and was not about to do the same. He was spending the money that should have been used for tuition on his drinking habit. Mercifully, he started drinking at dusk but remained sober all day. He was a disciplined man.

During my five years at that school, I discovered I enjoyed

design and worked diligently to improve my skills. The dean, who participated in juries reviewing projects, saw my potential at the end of my first year and asked me to join the staff in his private practice at a nominal salary. I was excited at the unexpected prospect of being trained to work on actual projects and, at the same time, being paid to do it. However, the schedule was grueling. Six days a week I took the street car from school then transferred to a bus to get home, had dinner, took the bus to the dean's office downtown and worked from 5:00 to 9:00 PM. When the deadline for one of my school projects approached, I had to travel back to school after finishing my work at the office and spend the night working on my project for two or three nights in a row. Several of my classmates also worked on their projects throughout the night. Sometimes, after working three or four hours, we joked around to keep our sanity and break the monotony.

On one occasion, around 1 or 2 o'clock in the morning, I felt very hungry, so I asked my friend Salah if he felt the same. He said yes, and we headed out to find something to eat. At that time of the morning, almost everything was closed. We walked and walked until we found a lighted shop. It was in the native quarter and that "restaurant," which was named "Abdul Salaam" (Abdul's for short), looked really derelict but we were desperate. We asked the waiter what food was available. He mentioned something that sounded edible. Apéritifs were usually free, and he brought a saucer of yellowish thick liquid along with some pita bread. We looked at each other quizzically, wondering how to deal with it. Hunger is a great motivator and we rashly dipped a piece of bread in "IT". The moment it hit our taste buds, we knew we had made a grave mistake. It tasted so bad it made our eyes water. We gave up after a few more dips (we were that hungry) and dreaded what our order would be like.

The main course was highly forgettable but we would always remember "IT" the so-called appetizer. When we returned, the rest of the group asked how we fared. Salah told them, "We found a great place to eat. You should try it sometime," and told them where we had gone. I said, "I'm not sure about the appetizer, though." Salah continued to expand on the story. When they interrupted to ask what "IT" was, Salah stopped long enough to say with a straight face, *"Khara,"* meaning "sh--". They asked, "What was it, really?" He repeated the expletive and continued as if he had said nothing out of the ordinary. Finally, he leveled with them. From then on, whenever a member of the group went to some below-par eating establishment, he would say, "I went to Abdul's".

When exhaustion set in, some of us retired to a dark studio and took a nap to prepare for the following day. A member of our group, on his way back from the restroom, discovered that another sleeper had left a stinking pair of socks in one of the classrooms. He told the rest of us, "I was walking by the door of a seminar room and noticed all the rats (rats sometimes raced across the floor at night) were running out of that room, holding their noses!" When I investigated, I found those socks next to Nadir (a sleeping upper classman)." Of course, we couldn't let that occasion go unnoticed, so we affixed those socks to the bulletin board with a funny comment about their owner. When that individual awoke, he looked for his socks everywhere then asked if we had seen them. Of course, we professed complete ignorance. It was only after other students arrived and started laughing at the comment on the bulletin board that he discovered where his socks went.

One night around 3 or 4 o'clock in the morning, we decided to stop work and roam through the school. An irresponsible classmate who was always looking for mischief said, "Suppose there is a fire. What will we do?" Before anybody could say a thing, he picked up a fire extinguisher mounted on the wall, upended it and shook it, spraying the whole stair with foam. He was the most irresponsible and useless person I have ever known. He convinced gullible students to do his drawings for him and lived for the excitement of the moment. We scampered back to our classroom and resumed work on our projects as if nothing had happened. Later that day, one of us had to admit that we did it when he was questioned by a member of the faculty about it. We all had to pay the penalty of cleaning up the mess.

On another occasion, around 4 o'clock in the morning, we decided to call it a day and went into a studio which had a warm, fuzzy, fabric backdrop and a still-life scene composed of fruits and pots. There were easels with unfinished oil paintings depicting that scene. Having been up all night, I thought we were going to lie down on the floor as usual and take a nap before classes began, but that same trouble-maker had another plan. He said, "Let's eat those bananas and apples." We were cold and hungry and his suggestion sounded awfully good. The reader can imagine what happened next. The following day there was a furor when the art students came back to finish their drawings and found the backdrop on the floor where we had left it after using it as a combination sheet/blanket, and the only evidence of the still life was the pots and the skins and cores of the fruit. During the day, the public address system announced that all studios would be locked at night as a result of that caper. Our group said, "Oh, rats!" and decided to refrain from spending the night at school lest they accuse us "innocents" of such dastardly deeds.

The School of Fine Arts was modeled after its French counterpart, *L'école des Beaux Arts* in Paris. Each year, the school opened its doors to the public and showed off the best projects drawn that year. It was a festive occasion, like a carnival. I remember in particular a very talented senior art student who specialized in drawing caricatures. He would dash off a sketch of any unfortunate professor who happened to pass by. Those sketches left no doubt about who the victim was. The school also conducted a parade in the neighborhood with great fanfare, complete with drums. Art students used papier-mâché floats and multi-colored banners to draw attention and show their creativity. It was an exciting time. Egyptians delight in making fun of politicians and crafting veiled jokes about tough times.

Trips

Between semesters, my classmates and I went camping or visited interesting destinations. On one of those trips we went to Mersa Matruh, a village on the Mediterranean near the border with Libya. We spent about seven hours on the slow train from Cairo to reach it. During the trip, we saw a large, ham-fisted Egyptian Bedouin (the Bedouins are nomadic tribes inhabiting the western desert) accompanying a Libyan prisoner in shackles. The first guy must have been a member of some plainclothes border guard unit accompanying the Libyan to execute a deportation order. They talked for a while in an unintelligible tongue and then all of a sudden, the guard struck the prisoner's face forcefully, violently turning his head and almost giving him a whiplash. The Libyan let off a stream of quick, unintelligible gibberish that elicited another tremendous slap. This was repeated several times before the prisoner quieted down to avoid being slapped to death. Of course, nobody interfered.

Marsa Matruh's permanent population was composed of flies, donkeys, Arab nomads and a few government employees. It had world-class beaches, white sand and turquoise water protected by a barrier reef. We pitched a tent on the beach and had a great time swimming, preparing our meals and exploring. It was a carefree time although it was rumored there were sharks in the water. During one of our forays on the beaches, we discovered a tunnel labyrinth carved in the soft rock with openings for gun turrets and were told it was Rommel's headquarters during the war. It was thrilling to come in touch with history although that tunnel was now used as an unofficial latrine and stank to high heaven. On another exploratory trip, we came upon the rusty hulk of a ship that had foundered against a rocky shore far away from the beaches. It was probably a relic from WWII, and we were surprised when an Arab caretaker who was guarding it emerged from its interior. I have no idea how this guy survived during storms. After I started working for the government, that town was not as enjoyable because I had to work there under less than ideal conditions. More on that later.

Another trip was to visit the Pyramids at Giza, a town across the Nile from Cairo. These gigantic tombs are awesome to behold. No picture can do them justice. Our group decided to climb the Great Pyramid of Khufu (the largest of a group of three at that site) . My first time to climb the exterior of it was a terrifying experience. Each stone is approximately 30 to 36 inches in height. Each subsequent stone course is inset from the one below, forming a ledge about 8 to 10 inches wide, which was barely enough to accommodate a sideways foothold for reaching the top of the stone above. To make matters more difficult, these ledges were covered with a thick layer of fine sand or dust, increasing the danger of slipping and falling. Trying to balance on these narrow ledges was hard on my muscles and nerves.

Halfway up, I became a nervous wreck and began shaking like a leaf, wishing I hadn't embarked on this hazardous venture. I looked down and found that descending would be even scarier. I had no choice but to continue to the top, hope to make it and after resting, things would look better. The view from the top was panoramic. I saw the whole city of Cairo from that lofty position. It was almost worth the effort and the anguish that I felt during the climb. After I rested, I was somehow able to gather enough nerve to get to the ground. I didn't like that feeling of utter terror, so I decided to do it again on subsequent trips. In all, I climbed that pyramid four times, and after the last climb, the technique became so familiar, I was able to jump from stone to stone on the way down. This experience taught me to face my fears and get the best of them. One of our group found a shady cavity about one third of the way up, sat there smoking a cigarette and told the rest, "I am going to stay here. When you reach the top, tell me what you have seen and whether it was worth it!" I felt sorry for him. He missed the thrill of discovery and the great feeling one gets after facing a big challenge and emerging triumphant.

Discouraged in Fayoum (I am fourth from the left)

We also climbed the Great Pyramid on the inside to reach King Cheops's burial chamber. The air inside was barely breathable and reeked with the sweat of people making the steep and arduous effort to climb the ramp in the poorly ventilated shaft. The chamber was located about halfway up the pyramid. When my friends and I saw the gigantic granite stones measuring approximately 15' x 7' forming the ceiling, a member of our group who was a wag said, "I can imagine when those Ancient Egyptians placed each stone in its final position, they must have had quite a celebration and brought Frank Sinatra to belt out one of his songs!" (Yes, Frank Sinatra's fame had reached Egypt.) Climbing the two lower pyramids adjoining the Great Pyramid was not allowed because they were less "safe." Today, I am not sure climbing any pyramid on the outside is still permitted.

On another trip, we took the train to an oasis called Fayoum about 50 miles south of Cairo. We camped next to the lake. When we started to erect our two tents, we had to clear some rocks and noticed that whenever we lifted a rock, a small scorpion scampered away. While this was alarming, we amused ourselves by lifting each rock and killing the critter below it. Unfortunately, one of us got stung and we had to bundle him up and take him to the local hospital where they administered a disinfectant and gave him antivenin and tetanus shots. Luckily, bites from small scorpions are usually not fatal. After a couple of days, we ran out of food and decided to take the bus back to Cairo. While waiting for the bus, we became exceedingly hungry, took stock and discovered we had only two cans of boiled spinach without any flavoring or anything to make the contents edible. We had no choice and, after opening them, we drained them and ate the contents....UGH! That was the icing on the cake for a trip that was the only failure among all the ones we participated in.

The last trip I remember was a train trip to Luxor. Our group stayed in a budget hotel. When I say budget, I mean "Budget" with a capital B. It was winter and, while the weather was pleasant and warm during the day, it turned windy and very chilly at night. The windows were not air-tight and poorly installed. It felt like an arctic gale-force wind was blowing on our beds. We asked for extra covers and covered the foot boards to reduce the speed of air against our bodies and bundled up with all our clothes on under the covers. We posed for a "formal old-timey picture" like the official portraits of government employees posed for in olden times. We assumed a serious demeanor but burst out laughing at the moment the camera clicked.

At the hotel in Luxor, I am seated second from left

After we had a full day of sightseeing, we gathered at the hotel restaurant, where we chose an entrée and a soup. The menu did not specify what kind of soup it was but we reasoned that it would warm us up. After ingesting some of the liquid, one of us noticed his had a protein bonus. It looked like a tick. We called the waiter and showed it to him. He denied it was an insect and said it was a bit of the meat. We suspected that the soup was camel soup (yes, camel meat is eaten by poor people in Egypt). We refrained from eating there after that.

Chapter 6
AT WORK

Upon graduation from college, I reviewed the employment picture in Cairo and came to the realization that architectural firms there were rare, probably only ten or fifteen at that time, which employed mostly Moslem architects. New graduates usually found employment with various government departments and municipalities in a few major cities.

After I applied at the Cairo Municipality, all hiring came to a grinding halt until political power sorted itself out. A year later, after living from hand to mouth on my meager pay from my night job at the dean's office and a little help from my brothers, the ban on hiring was lifted and I received a letter informing me I was hired. I was elated and imagined I would be assigned to design buildings and demonstrate the talent I had spent five years training for. My joy at getting the job was short-lived, however, when I discovered my assignment entailed applying zoning rules to new subdivisions, no design talent required. My immediate bosses were Copts who treated me as a colleague. The head of the department was a Moslem who treated me like a nobody.

The job required me to deal with irate land owners who did not like the rules. After about a year, I was transferred to the Department of Property Appropriations. The work required me to go to slum areas scheduled for clearance to provide land necessary for constructing the new highway bordering the river

Nile. The tenements were old and decrepit, and the tenants lived in squalor. My task required me to compute the area of each floor, multiply it by the number of floors then multiply the total area by the price per square meter assessed by the estimator to arrive at the total compensation for the homeowners. It was exhausting work, entailing numerous ascents and descends of rickety stairs three or four floors high. The hovels were also depressing, unhygienic and smelly due to overcrowded toilets that lacked maintenance. The other members of the staff extorted bribes from homeowners to inflate compensation estimates. That job did not relate to architecture either, and the department was staffed by minimally educated people, one of whom had dictatorial tendencies and treated the tenants like trash. I referred to him as the bulldozer.

When the highway was completed, I was glad to learn I would be transferred to the Building Permits Department. I was put in charge of issuing building permits and conducting inspections to assure no building was being erected without one. I thought, "Well, at least it has to do with building instead of demolition and it will familiarize me with the building code." The area assigned to me was the low-rise part of the city of Giza across the Nile from Cairo, a sizable area which would normally require two or three people with adequate transportation to do the work properly and in a timely fashion. While this new job was somewhat related to architecture, the department was manned by graduates of an unaccredited technical school. Most of them had cars and lived in villas, things almost nobody could afford on a government salary. I found out later they collected bribes to issue permits, even if the drawings conformed to the code. It is true graft and corruption are not unique to Egypt and that one can find it in any major city in the third world. The difference is that, in this department, the government employees made it obligatory for all building permit applicants to pay a bribe. A larger bribe was also exacted from those who built housing without a permit, to make the employee look the other way. The job also required me to write tickets to be delivered to owners who built without acquiring a license or deviated from the plans. I had to appear in court to testify against them if they refused to pay the fine or contested my findings. In other words, this was a really "fun" job.

The director of the department called a meeting of the newly hired college graduates and told us he wanted us to be diligent in applying the code to improve the reputation of the department. I could not imagine doing otherwise. I applied the code to the letter. When a set of plans landed on my desk, the person who applied for the permit would naturally assume I was on the take and brazenly open my desk drawer and put the customary bribe in. I would immediately take it out and patiently explain as I gave it back that I did not do that sort of thing. You should have seen the look on his face (most applicants were men), amazement and relief mixed with apprehension there might be complications that might be costly or delay construction.

In most cases, the deviations were minor and easily corrected. Sometimes the people whom the applicant had bribed before would try to intercede to make me change my mind, but I held firm because I could not, in good conscience, ignore the code requirements. Needless to say, this did not endear me to the rest of the employees. On one occasion, I did not approve a set of drawings for an apartment building because it deviated from code conformance. The owner, a woman (we rarely dealt with women) came to my desk in a rage, demanding I give my approval. My impression was she was coached by the guys in the next room. Normally, I would have reacted with anger at her insulting behavior. In this instance, I reacted calmly and invited her to take a seat across from me. Our conversation went something like this:

"I don't know why you have refrained from approving these drawings when my architect has assured me they conformed to the code."

"I have listed all the items that need modifications to come into conformance."

I explained each item and told her what would happen to the building if she did not make the change. I also explained that if she did not do it, somebody from our department may do an inspection of the building after it was built and require her to make the change at greater cost, not counting the fine that went along with non-conformance.

"Now I understand. Thank you. I was misled by my architect."

"You're welcome. These changes are minor and should not require too much work or time from your architect."

I cannot explain what prompted me to become calm in the face of that unwarranted and undeserved attack except to say that God must have guided me in dealing with this situation.

During that time, most building permit applications for churches were refused on technicalities that would not be enforced if the building were a mosque or assigned to a different usage. It was frustrating for me to review the drawings, find they were in conformance and have the approved drawings disappear in a bureaucratic quagmire. This, however, was par for the course for a government that professes to be "tolerant" concerning Christians, but practices the opposite. If, by a fluke, a church got built or an existing building was converted to a church, a large mosque would be built in close proximity to it. It would be equipped with the customary high-volume loudspeakers to broadcast the call to prayer or readings from the Qur'an during church services, making it very difficult to hear what was said inside.

At the building permit department, my refusal to accept "donations" from people applying for a permit really upset the employees on the take because it gave the applicants the wrong idea that they could get a permit without paying the others their usual cut. They also resented the fact that a juicy part of the city, which could have been added to their areas to increase their income, was assigned to me. So they wrote an anonymous complaint to the newly formed Government Investigations Administration, which was established after people complained about the rampant graft. The department was established for the purpose of cleaning up corruption. It was manned by recent graduates of the law school to investigate corrupt practices and refer those found to be guilty to the Department of Justice to receive harsh punishment. The complaint stated that a building was being erected without a permit. It was located in an alley branching from another alley on the outskirts of the four-square-mile area of closely built slums assigned to me. It intimated that I ignored that building because I was bribed to look the other way. These anonymous complaints were always taken very seriously.

As a result, I was summoned to a waiting room in the investigations building in Cairo. No seating was provided and I was kept standing for an hour before being summoned to the presence of a wet-behind-the-ears lawyer who treated me as if I were guilty of the most heinous crime. After asking me a bunch of insulting questions, he issued a verdict that I was grossly negligent. He didn't ask whether I was guilty or not or if I had any rebuttals. I was prepared to explain how impossible it was to uncover every instance of non-conformance in such a large area using the limited means of transportation at my disposal. The only transportation available to do the inspections was a motorcycle driven by a low-paid employee, with an open sidecar where I sat. It could not be used in inclement weather, or if the driver was on sick leave or vacation or if the motorcycle had a mechanical problem.

None of these factors mattered. I returned to the office fuming. The next day I started early and combed the outlying area for any sign of illegal construction. I must have written fifty citations on that day, finishing at five o'clock without a lunch break. When I got home, I discovered I was covered with fleas which infested that poor neighborhood. All the illegal builders flocked to the office the following week, making loud protestations. The director called me in to ask me to ease up in the future. I told him about my experience at the investigator's office. He must have reached the correct conclusion that I was not going to stop. Shortly afterwards, I was transferred to the Construction Department in Cairo, another department entrusted with the supervision of construction of low-income housing. At least this was an area where I could gain some professional experience, practice interaction with construction crews and learn the construction jargon.

About a year after my transfer, as the construction job I was supervising neared completion, strings were pulled by people who had the "right connections," e.g., being Moslem, for my position. Contrary to the terms of my employment contract which specified I was employed by the Cairo Municipality and could be transferred only within that administration, I found myself facing an order to report for work in a small remote town in another state called Beni-Suef which was far away from my family. It required a two-and-a-half-hour train trip one way. That town was without any of the amenities I had gotten used to, such as movie theaters, restaurants, parks, easy transportation as well as the supplemental income from my evening job, etc. It was a triple whammy, a substantial added expense for transportation, loss of one-third of my income from my evening job and less time to spend with the family and for entertainment.

Such an order could not be contested by a Copt who had no connections even if he was the sole provider for his widowed sister and her offspring. I had no option but to comply. My salary was the equivalent of $100 a month. The standard of living was lower than that enjoyed by those living in the western world. Still, it was a hand-to-mouth existence with no room for anything but the bare necessities. I just hoped none of us would fall sick since health insurance did not exist in Egypt. This move made things even more difficult since the terms of employment for a government employee required one to reside in the city where one works. That would have meant additional expenditure for renting inferior housing and living in a town without any kind of recreational activities or entertainment.

After considering the issue, I decided to refrain from adhering to the residency requirement and bought a monthly train pass to commute daily. This required me to get up at 5:30 AM, get dressed, have breakfast and make the 2½-hour bus and train trip to arrive about thirty minutes late. I did not take time out for lunch and worked hard until 5 o'clock then caught the train and made the 2½-hour return trip to arrive home around 7:30 PM. I felt like a slave enduring 14½-hour work days but had what can be described as job security, because no Moslem would be willing to take up my impossible workload. To save on expenses, I went once a week to the local farmers' market at the center of town to buy a hunk of meat that would last the family till the following market day. I had to carry the crudely packaged bundle on the train and bus until I got home. In conversations with my fellow passengers, I discovered that most were Christians who commuted back and forth between Cairo and Beni-Suef. I remember in particular a doctor who told us his boss had the following conversation with him:

"Didn't your Jesus prophesy the advent of the prophet Mohammad?"
"He sure did. He mentioned that after Him (Jesus) will come many false prophets and charlatans and said don't listen to them."
This was a gutsy and foolhardy statement which, though it was quoted from the Bible, must have caused him problems afterward.

My new job entailed inspecting construction work on government buildings to make sure the contractor was conforming to the drawings and specifications. It required travel to three small towns where several types of projects were being constructed to provide services that were lacking during the former regime. The local building administration had two vehicles to serve the three architects assigned to different areas of that province. One of those vehicles was assigned to the director of the department. It was used mostly to run errands for his family. The other was not always available, either because the driver was on sick leave or it was being used by another architect. When the car broke down, transportation was provided by the contractor, who was not required by his contract to do so. This meant I would be indebted to him since he would be doing me a favor. It also meant I could not go except when it was convenient for him to do so. At one time, I was assigned to monitor sixteen projects which included two-story hen houses, schools, multi-family housing and other building types scattered among the three towns. Inspections could not be postponed when a car was unavailable because I would be held responsible for delaying the construction program to implement the ridiculously hasty progress mandated by politics.

A resident representative of the administration (a low-paid, barely literate clerk) was assigned to each site to make sure any corrections or omissions noted by me were addressed. In theory, this seems like a good system. In reality, on-site representatives were usually bribed by the contractor to look the other way while the workers did something illegal like removing reinforcing steel from the forms where concrete was to be poured or lessening the amount of cement in the mortar mix or other creative machinations the contractor would come up with to reduce costs and maximize profits. Of course, all these shenanigans occurred after I finished my inspection and left. If anything went wrong as a result of that cheating, the outcome could be interpreted to mean that I had not checked the reinforcement or concrete mix. This would become grounds for bypassing me for promotion or it could delay or cancel the rare and meager raise (about .5% of my salary) which was usually scheduled every three years. It could also result in a transfer to an even less desirable location.

In the meantime, another employee of the Department of Building, who was on loan as a liaison to the governor's office and who commuted with me on the train, told me the governor was looking for an architect to design a new governorate (State House) for the province. He told me he would nominate me for that assignment. A couple of days later, I was summoned to the governor's office and had the honor of meeting the governor who handed me a site map and a list of what he would like to see included in the building. I was elated because I would finally be involved in design, something I really liked. Unfortunately, I found out this assignment was to be in addition to my regular work. That meant I would do the sketching, drafting and making presentations to the governor between my primary assignment and field trips as well as doing the drawings after I got home exhausted from the daily commute. While this was extremely taxing, I was finally enjoying what I was doing.

I did a preliminary design that was reviewed by the governor and approved. I then made the minor modifications he asked for and developed the final construction drawings. He asked me to take the drawings to an architectural college professor friend of his for review.

Partial picture of Beni Suef State House

It was midsummer and his friend taught at a university in Asyut, a city in the hottest part of the country. I hated going there at that time of year. I took the train and rented a room in the only hotel in town, a primitive structure without air conditioning. I stayed the night in a stiflingly hot room also occupied by swarms of giant mosquitoes which dive-bombed me all night and drained a sizable amount of my blood. The mosquito netting over the bed did not deter them one bit. I suspect the netting was full of holes I couldn't see in the gloom. I kept my appointment the next morning with the professor, who reviewed the drawings and approved them. As soon as the meeting ended, I went to the station and took the next train back to Cairo. I arrived home earlier than usual that day and slept for ten hours.

Finally, the building was finished and the governor was pleased with the result. To show his satisfaction, he issued an order to award me the lordly sum of 50 Egyptian pounds (approximately $90 at the going rate of exchange at the time) as compensation for my working overtime and doing the work of a whole team of architects single-handed. This unprecedented and unexpected windfall caused extreme envy among the employees both at the governor's office and in the building department where I worked. The former group decided to retaliate if a chance presented itself. That chance was not long in coming.

One day a general inspector from the Building Ministry in Cairo arrived to investigate a complaint about a four-story courthouse building under my purview that had experienced a condition which can be described as an imitation of the leaning tower of Pisa. Whoever reported it never told me about it. I had not anticipated such a catastrophe. That inspector did not have any forensic qualifications or special technical training to investigate building problems. He was pressed for time to catch the next train to Cairo. After a cursory visual inspection which lasted all of ten minutes, he reached the erroneous conclusion that the soil stratum on which the foundations rested was too weak to carry the building load. I tried to explain what the real reason was but, through his purported superior "knowledge" (he had graduated from my alma mater), he ignored my explanations and wrote his report accordingly.

Unlike in the United States and Europe, there were no soils engineers or test borings to determine the load-bearing capacity of the different soil strata. This determination was performed by the supervising architect rubbing the dirt in his hand, putting on a sagacious demeanor and stating that, in his experience, such-and-such depth is the layer at which the digging should stop. In most cases this so-called test worked due to sheer luck. The real reason for the courthouse's failure, based on my inspection, was the hasty piling of dirt fill around the concrete foundation footings before concrete was poured in the columns. Since the forms around the columns were assembled from much-used lumber with gaps caused by damaged boards, some of the dirt would have accumulated at the bottom of some of the columns, creating a dirt pocket where the concrete should have been. This was done after I had left the site and should have been stopped by the resident observer since it did not conform to the specs. To reinforce my conclusion, some of the reinforcement could be seen bent at the bottom of the columns on the lower side of the building, causing the structure to lean. The bending occurred because the load could not be carried by the steel alone in the absence of concrete.

As a result of the erroneous report, I was transferred to Mersa Matruh, the same small town on the Mediterranean where I and my camping group in college had gone on one of our summer vacations. Most of the Egyptian nomads who lived in that town hated to work. When fishing, they used gelignite extracted from unexploded bombs left over from the war to stun the fish, then collected them from the surface. Of course, some of them paid the price of their laziness through missing arms. Their main source of income was the smuggling of Japanese electronic equipment and other contraband from Libya. They used donkeys that were trained to memorize the route and then travel on their own. When the border police made one of their infrequent raids, they confiscated the contraband but couldn't find anybody to arrest, so they arrested the donkeys and auctioned them off. Of course, the smugglers, who didn't want to train rookie donkeys, bought them back.

Everybody benefited: The smugglers were able to continue smuggling, raising their prices fractionally to make up for the loss; the cops reported the success of the raid and pocketed the income from the sale of part of the loot on the black market, and the government employees bought contraband, unavailable in the rest of the country, for very good prices. Egypt had stopped imports of non-essential merchandise (meaning non-military) at the time, and whatever was available on the legitimate market was inferior merchandise imported from the Eastern Block and taxed beyond the average person's ability to afford. Even the governor's aide flaunted an FM radio and asked me what FM meant. I hadn't a clue... and still don't.

During the summer, the population quadrupled in Mersa Matruh. People came from many parts of Egypt to enjoy the white sand beaches which, at that time, were not as crowded as those in Alexandria. It took eight hours by "express" train or twelve hours by slow train from Cairo to reach that destination or a six-hour trip in an air-conditioned bus if you were able to pay much more. That meant I had to rent an apartment because commuting was out of the question. I inquired about lodging at the local building administration where I was supposed to start working. I was told by the unsympathetic director, who was my new boss, that it was the tourist season and no apartments were available. I asked him what he expected me to do under the circumstances. He told me he was not responsible and suggested I buy a tent and camp on the beach until the end of the season! This really upset me. Not only was I transferred to that God-forsaken place, but I had to live like a pup in a tent. To make this suggestion even more annoying, the nearest store that would sell such an item was in Alexandria, six hours away!

I spent that night at a run-down "hotel." In the morning I took the return train to Cairo, went the next day to the Ministry of Construction and asked to see the minister. After waiting for a couple of hours, I was allowed to meet briefly with the deputy minister who told me he would talk to the director of the local administration. In the meantime, he advised me to go back and assume my new position. I got the message: *Do as you are told, this is your problem, you solve it.* If I went on strike or refused to obey, I would be called to appear before a young lawyer in the Investigations Administration to be accused of gross dereliction of duty or worse. Resignation was illegal and even if it weren't, where would I work after that? This was the most aggravating situation I had encountered yet. Not only had I been transferred to the ends of the earth away from everybody I knew but I had become homeless.

The next day, after buying a pup tent, I boarded the train for the long trip to the seashore and erected it on the beach in the area assigned to camping. Of course, I had to pay a rental fee for the space. Being a pup (except for the bark) is a demeaning and ridiculous situation, even by Egyptian standards. I tried to make the best of a bad situation by taking a dip in the sea at the end of each day followed by a shower. When the rest of the staff learned about this arrangement, the director felt compelled to find an apartment to accommodate me.

From that time onward, I decided to find ways to get around the ban on resignations and travel abroad. When my two-week vacation time came, I applied to get an exit visa to make a pilgrimage to the holy sites in Jerusalem. This was a one-time exemption from the ban on travel that was allowed for

Christians. Many of the other employees said I was doing this to get out of the country permanently. I denied it, of course, but it was the actual motivation. I did go to Jerusalem which was, at the time, ruled by Jordan. However, I was afraid to deviate from visiting the sites because I was almost certain there were government spies among the group of Christian pilgrims in the guided tour I was with. If I visited the American embassy to apply for refugee status, I might be arrested when I returned. I made the best of it by praying fervently for deliverance when I visited the Church of the Nativity and the Stations of the Cross.

The author (in dark clothes) explaining a project to the governor and the construction minister. The head of our department is at the far left

While working in Mersa Matruh was, on the whole, depressing because of my isolation from family and the lack of any social life, I had one moment of excitement when the Construction Minister from Cairo made an inspection visit to the town. He, the Governor of the province and the Director of Housing toured several sites including numerous projects I was in charge of. I explained the building processes and stages. They were accompanied by aides and a photographer from *Al Ahram*, the

Cairo newspaper who snapped pictures. That was a new experience for me.

Chapter 7

THE LIGHT AT THE END OF THE TUNNEL

After working for three years inspecting construction sites and supervising two other architects, the country's defeat in the Six-day War with Israel in 1967 resulted in forcing the government to end restrictions on resignations and travel to other countries. I decided this was the opportunity I was waiting for since my teens. My prayers were answered in God's appropriate time. I knew what I had to do next without any trace of doubt or hesitation. I applied for emigration before the government changed its new policy (which it did a few years later). When I told my friends and family, those who knew what I had been going through congratulated me and wished me luck. Those who didn't tried to dissuade me, saying I had a good, secure position and asking me why I wanted to risk all that. What I described in these past chapters was reason enough for me. The lack of freedoms and employment choices, the separation of the sexes, the discrimination and low standard of living were but a few of these reasons. Besides, I could see that my future in that country was nothing to look forward to.

I knew there would be quite a risk of failure to get an exit visa from the Egyptian bureaucrats and an entry visa to the United States was iffy but, I also knew if I didn't try, I would regret it for the rest of my life. I also knew that in the US I would not be discriminated against because of my religious beliefs, would have better opportunities for employment and advancement, as well as have a chance for a social life. While this is true in general terms, at least, if I was discriminated against in the US, it would be because I didn't measure up or because I wasn't clearly understood rather than because I was born a Christian. Life for a foreign national has its challenges in any country he or she opts to emigrate to.

One of the terms imposed on prospective emigrants, after the new easing of travel restrictions, was that the employee must tender his resignation before applying for the exit visa. Due to the ruined economy, no other employment was available if I failed to acquire the exit visa or should my application for immigration to the US be denied by the embassy. This made me feel as if I was teetering at the edge of a precipice. Did those awful odds deter me from seeking to leave the country? Not in the least. I tendered my resignation which was reluctantly accepted by the director since they were short-handed. I felt sorry for his predicament but it couldn't be helped. Oddly enough, the US Congress passed legislation canceling the quota system limiting the number of immigrants from certain countries, including Egypt, and the only requirement was that an applicant had to have a college degree. It is amazing how God works things out.

The next day, I made my final trip to Cairo from Mersa Matruh and applied at the American Embassy for an immigrant visa. I asked about the required documentation and was given a list which included a passport picture, my curriculum vitae, a birth certificate, and a health certificate providing proof of vaccinations and other health information, and sponsorship from a relative in the US. I contacted my brother Wilson for the sponsorship. After a few weeks, he finally sent it. After I received the embassy's approval, I had to go from office to office, petitioning hostile bureaucrats in the Egyptian exit visa department to move my request along. I was determined not to pay any bribes and that was part of the reason the process was as hard and slow as it was. The Egyptian government employees who gave me the most grief with obstacle after obstacle, made it difficult to get the coveted exit visa. Finally in 1968, all the exit documents were in my hands. This process had taken a year.

With the visas in hand, I bought a travel package which included a one-way plane ticket to New York with two-day stops in both London and Paris, cities I had always wanted to see. After interminable delays at the crowded Cairo airport, the time finally came for the flight to take off. The family bade me a teary goodbye and I proceeded to the Boeing 707 belonging to the Greek airline I had made my reservation on. After a short wait the plane revved its engines and I became excited at the prospect of gaining my long postponed freedom. That was the first time I had boarded a plane. The plane taxied to the runway and gathered speed for the take-off. My excitement and elation increased; however, the plane started slowing down, made a U-turn and came back slowly to the terminal. I was flabbergasted. Had the government changed its mind about allowing people to leave? Were the secret police going to yank me off the flight and drag me kicking and screaming to some concentration camp for some unknown reason? Fortunately, none of my fears came to pass. The pilot's voice came over the public address system and stated in Greek-accented English that the plane had developed a flat tire and we needed to deplane until they fixed it. I suspect they had to fly in a new tire from Greece because it took more than three hours to change that flat. Finally, we re-boarded and took off without further complication. I had chosen a window seat which allowed me to watch the ground until I saw the Mediterranean below. I felt like dancing in the aisle. My lifelong ordeal in this socialist "Workers' Paradise" of discrimination was finally coming to an end. At last I was leaving my "Egypt for Romance!" for good. I cannot describe the feeling of euphoria I experienced at the thought of finally being free.

CONCLUSION – Part 1

In retrospect, considering my life as a whole, I reach the conclusion that God has always reached His hand to my family and provided a graceful exit from every sticky situation I found myself in. He was there for me when I was about to be thrashed to a pulp in primary school by making the stone-faced headmaster tap me on the shoulder and say, "You may go." He was there to prevent me from running away from home to escape my brother Amin's attacks. He was there when He inspired Wilson to move our family away from the bombings during WWII, and He was there for my favorite brother, Naguib, by allowing him to leave the country before the Six-day War. He prevented me from reacting to an unwarranted verbal attack by the irate woman applying for a building permit. He extracted me from jobs I abhorred before I gave in to despair. Finally, He forced President Nasser to loosen the constraints against emigration so I could seek a better life in the US. God is gracious and merciful.

While I have concentrated on many negative experiences during my narrative, I must stress the fact that my life in Egypt was not completely devoid of happy moments. As a child, I enjoyed my family's hockey and ping-pong games as well as my model airplane hobby. I also loved the camaraderie of my Moslem classmates in college when we went on camping trips, especially my best friend, Salah, a Moslem who had a good sense of humor and no prejudice against anyone. I also have fond memories of my childhood in Alexandria where we used to frolic in the sea, and the delicious food my mother cooked. Most of these experiences, however, occurred before the Nasser regime came to power and before my awful experiences after joining the work force. I bear no malice toward my former country or its people and wish it would allow all ethnic groups to be treated equally and live in peace without discrimination, instead of falsely claiming that they are "tolerant" toward them and looking the other way when extremists go on a rampage against them.

Egypt has always been the leader of the Arab World, even after the rise in oil prices which allowed the countries that produce oil for export to advance materially. The money allowed those countries to build universities and high-rises, making them seem more important in the region. However, they do not have the rich history, cultural heritage and the arts Egypt is known for. Egypt has a vibrant theater and movie industry, its music and films are popular among its neighbors, and its population has a great sense of humor. It boasts world-class beaches and scuba-diving sites. It has a well-established judicial system administered by judges without the benefit of juries, which may or may not be a good thing, depending on which system invites more abuse. From what I have observed since I came to this country, our system is not perfect either.

Needless to mention, my ancestors, the Ancient Egyptians, produced the awesome pyramids and the famous temples at Luxor, including the vast Karnak Temple complex, that attract tourists from all over the world. Its weather, while hot in summer, is relatively mild and stable the rest of the year. It is the only country in the Middle East which has signed a peace treaty with Israel and abided by it. However, like all countries in that area, it was ruled by an autocrat who got elected using fraudulent means (things have improved after the ouster of extreme and fanatical Morsy regime). The country has tremendous potential for solving its substantial problems if it had leadership with vision and a properly educated majority. Attending religious schools (or *madrassahs* as they are referred to in the US) should not qualify as an education.

It is my sincere hope that God would inspire the people and their government to stem the tide of prejudicial treatment against the Christian minority. I also wish they would realize it is in their best interest to utilize the Copts' talents rather than make life difficult for them and impede their progress. The Moslem Brotherhood fanatical regime was elected with the support of President Obama, President Morsy of the Brotherhood mismanaged the country so badly that he was toppled as a result and elected President El Sisi who is taking the country in the right direction, finally. Of course this does not mean that fanaticism has been vanquished. At least, it is no longer government policy to side with the fanatics. If left unchecked, those same fanatics will eventually turn against the government and topple it, as happened after President Sadat appeased them and was assassinated as a result. I am not optimistic about the country's future or the future of my relatives who still remain. The whole Middle East is currently in turmoil because of that nihilistic fanaticism.

PART 2

A NEW BEGINNING

Chapter 1
FREEDOM AT LAST

I emigrated from Egypt in 1968 with $200 in my pocket, the maximum amount of hard currency allowed for travelers leaving the country at the time. Needless to say, it was utterly inadequate to start a new life in America. My brother Wilson, who had been living in the US for some time, met me at LaGuardia Airport in New York and hailed a taxi to his home in New Jersey. He suggested that I apply for a job in one of the architectural offices but, I was dedtermined to get to know how architecture was practiced in the U.S. before I started work. So, he let me stay with his family for a few days, and helped me apply at several universities as well as took care of my expenses during my stay. He told me that he had talked with an acquaintance in Texas who was studying for his PhD who agreed to present a copy of my credentials at the UT School of Architecture and follow up the process to ascertain that my application would be reviewed quickly. In approximately ten days, I received a conditional approval from the University of Texas at Austin. This was great news, because I had seen all the sights accessible by walking and by bus from New Jersey to the multi-story Port Authority parking terminus in New York a couple of times, and walked miles and miles to see the city. I was beginning to wonder what God had in store for me.

Before I booked my flight from Egypt, I had shipped a large bag that contained all my mementoes, treasured possessions, and things that had sentimental value for me, using the same Greek airline I flew on. When my flight reached LaGuardia, I inquired about my shipped bag and was told it hadn't arrived yet. A couple of days later, I called and was informed thieves had broken into the airline's baggage storage facility and stolen many items, including my bag. They said they were in the process of determining the compensation and asked me to list the contents of the bag and estimate the value of each item on the list. I was devastated and asked my brother what to do. Wilson told me to list the contents, and ask for whatever I thought they were worth to me. I listed them as best I could remember, and estimated the total value at $600. After several back and forth letters, the airline stopped answering. I suspect they reached the conclusion that I wasn't going to sue them, and that it was safe to drop the subject without any fear of consequences. They were correct in that assumption because I didn't have the wherewithal to hire a lawyer, but I was deeply disappointed and upset at their unconscionable and callous behavior.

Wilson and his wife, Ruth, bought me a windbreaker as a going-away present, purchased the plane ticket and drove me to Newark Airport where I boarded a Southwest Airlines flight to Austin. I was impressed by the beauty of the flight attendants in their colorful and skimpy shorts, their radiant smiles, and bubbly sense of humor which expressed a *joie-de-vivre* I had never encountered before. The flight went smoothly, and before I knew it, we touched down in sunny Austin. After I reclaimed my bag from the carousel, I hailed a cab and told the driver to take me to the cheapest hotel in town. He took me to the Alamo Hotel downtown (no longer in existence). I was reassured when the clerk told me the rate was $5 a night. That was a relief because with my limited funds, I could almost hear the "ka-ching" of the cash register deducting $5 from the $170 or so which remained from my nest egg after paying the cab fare and other expenses when I was in New Jersey. However, I became really worried about staying until I had a source of income and found something closer to the UT campus. I wanted to get information about lodgings from the admissions office right away, but it was Saturday night and I had to stay at the hotel until the office opened on Monday. That also meant I had to pay for food for two days before I had a chance to solve my cash problem. I could already feel my remaining cash melting away without any money replacing it, KA-CHING...KA-CHING.

That evening, I went for a walk downtown and was surprised to see swarms of crickets flying like Kamikaze bombers, crashing into walls, cars and people, including me. There were heaps of dead ones in the gutters, especially at the base of street lamps. I though I was under attack, and began to wonder what kind of place I had gotten myself into. I was not sure whether this occurred yearly, or happened just that once for my benefit. I hated this feature of the city and the fact that the streets were almost empty in the early evening. This was so different from Cairo where the streets came alive in the evening when people would shop and go to movies and just stroll at that time, the coolest part of the day.

Early Monday morning, I asked at the hotel desk for directions, then headed on foot for the University of Texas campus about a mile away. I went to the administration building and explained my predicament to a receptionist. She directed me to an administrator at the International Student Office. Mrs. King was a cheerful and sympathetic lady of about 40 who listened to my story and said, "I have just the solution for you." She made a call and told me that a Chinese student who had researched the housing adjacent to the campus would arrive shortly to advise me about the least expensive choices.

Chang Ling asked me what school I was going to attend and

drove me directly to a rooming house a couple of blocks from the School of Architecture. The owner, Mr. Nelson of the Nelson House showed me the one room that was available and said the monthly rent was $20. Now I knew I might survive for a little while until I found some kind of employment. After all, that was in 1968 and the dollar went much further then than it does now. Of course that rate was for a small room with a shared bath and a refrigerator with a frosted-over freezer on the stair landing. There were no cooking facilities, condemning me to only what I could fix: cold sandwiches. Ham sandwiches, to be precise. That was the only kind I was familiar with. I could not afford to buy something I might not like and be stuck with eating it.

The following day, I went to the School of Architecture and showed the receptionist the letter from the dean. She made a phone call and Dean Taniguchi came out of his office to meet me. I was surprised to find that the top man himself would meet me personally. He looked Japanese but had no accent, and we had a pleasant conversation. I expressed the desire to enroll as an undergraduate student so that I could study architecture as taught in the U.S. He told me that, with my qualifications and my sixteen years of experience in the field, it would not be appropriate to place me with recent high-school graduates. He suggested I enroll in the Master of Architecture program instead. I am glad he dissuaded me, since hob-nobbing with teenagers of the late '60s Vietnam protest era would have been quite a challenge.

My meeting with dean Taniguchi was a refreshing contrast to my experience in Egypt, where a dean is typically aloof and isolated from the student body so as to maintain an aura of importance and respect. He showed me where I would have my workstation in the graduate lab, which was, unfortunately, isolated from the rest of the school. There was nobody there at the time. I had hoped to mingle with other students to get more exposure to the culture and improve my language skills. I also hoped to eventually meet some nice coed to make life more interesting. After all I was 38 years old already and hadn't had any contact with members of the opposite sex. I was glad, however, that I was set to start my new life on a sound basis.

When I expressed my deep worry about stretching the remainder of my money to make ends meet, the dean assured me he would assign me as a Teaching Assistant (TA) which meant the bulk of my tuition fees would be waived. He also told me a TA position would pay minimum wage. At the time it was $2.65 an hour. I figured if I worked four hours a day, I would earn about $11.00. I did a quick calculation in my head and came to the conclusion that two days' earnings would pay my monthly rent. This allayed my fears about my immediate money crisis. However, I worried about the fact that I had never taught anything in my life and did not like confronting a group of people. Let's face it, I was a hopeless introvert in these new surroundings.

The dean concluded by inviting me to have coffee at Chambers, a coffee shop across the street from campus (on a recent visit, I was saddened to find that it had been replaced by another building). I thought it was a great honor to be invited by the dean. He asked me about my experience, what I hoped to accomplish and what area of study I would like to pursue. This was a question I didn't anticipate. A master's degree in Egypt was managed according to a fixed program. One didn't choose subjects. I asked him to explain how the program was conducted and he said, "Each student is assigned to a Graduate Student Adviser to council him or her on selecting courses that would be helpful to formulate the final thesis for the chosen subject."

"Thesis" was a word I was unfamiliar with. I looked it up later in the dictionary and understood roughly what it meant. In answer to his question, I said I was interested in housing. I found out later that most graduate students select a more challenging subject such as hospitals or labs or other complicated buildings to give them a leg up when they applied at offices specializing in that particular genre of buildings. I, instead, chose a building type I was familiar with. As chance would have it, Dean Taniguchi was a superb designer of residential architecture. He took me a few days later to an almost-finished house he had designed and explained the thinking behind certain unique features he had introduced.

During our conversation at Chambers, he told me about growing up in California, his family's internment in a concentration camp during WWII and his experience as a truck driver. I was amazed because, where I came from, non-professional work such as truck-driving is the exclusive realm of the uneducated lower class. I believe that he was talking about the days before he went to college and his method of saving enough money to pay tuition. Dean Taniguchi also told me about his father, Isamu Taniguchi, who was born in Japan and was interned during WWII along with the family. After the war, his father moved to Texas and raised cotton and vegetables. Being a master Japanese garden designer, he volunteered to design and construct the Japanese Garden at Zilker Park in Austin. The dean passed away a few years ago. He was a great humanitarian who assisted minorities when it was not fashionable to do so. I was gratified and astonished about his revelations to a stranger like me. It was much later when I realized that he must have noticed how unusually diffident I was and did what he could to put me at ease. He was a truly remarkable human being, and I consider myself privileged to have met him.

The following day, the school receptionist at the front desk told me Professor Mather had been assigned as my adviser. When I met him, he struck me as being a very easy person to get along with. However, his methodology of instruction was totally alien to what I expected. He told me to work on extremely boring geometries to define occupant densities, how many square feet are adequate to accommodate families of different sizes and income levels, how many houses of different sizes would fit on an acre, etc. While I did not enjoy that kind of research at the time, I did get familiar with thinking in square feet instead of metric dimensions. I also got trained in the methodology of conducting research to reach a certain goal (unfortunately, he didn't define that goal). This work became useful later-on when I started writing technical books on architecture.

One of Professor Mather's favorite words was "heuristic," a word I had never heard before or since. I always asked him to explain it. He patiently did, and I immediately forgot it. According to *Webster's Dictionary*, it means "of or relating to exploratory problem-solving techniques that utilize self-educating techniques (as the evaluation of feedback) to improve performance." Looking back, I reached the conclusion it was an accurate description of what he was trying to convey, but if I were in his shoes, I would never have used such a word when speaking to a foreign student. Come to think of it, I wouldn't use it even to a local.

The graduate lab had only one other student. He was from Taiwan and he felt extremely homesick and lonely. His language skills were limited and he was much younger than I. We had nothing in common, which made chit chat difficult. This did not help with my feelings of isolation. That fall semester finally came to an end and I was wondering what I would be directed to do next. Dean Taniguchi came to the rescue. He told me the university had received an invitation to participate in an international competition sponsored by Argentina to devise ways to solve the problem of housing in Third World countries using technology devised by industrialized nations. I expressed my concern that a project for an international competition may be too large an undertaking for one person with limited time and resources. He assured me the school would provide materials such as paper and sources of information as well as cover the cost of sending the drawings to Argentina, should my project be selected as UT's submission for the competition. He also stated that because the project was too large to finish within the time frame, I should do what I could and the professor would grade my effort and the work and research I did toward finding a solution would also be graded and count toward my degree. Under these circumstances, my fears were allayed. He gave me a copy of the entry materials. It gave particulars about the goals, the format and the stipulation that this work was to be performed solely by the student without any assistance from faculty. I said to myself: *Oh, wow, what kind of learning process is this? I am handed a huge project and told to handle it without any guidance or hint from a professor.*

During that semester, I was assigned as a Teaching Assistant to Professor Oswaldo (not his real name) who was from Mexico or Cuba. He taught first-year students the proper way to hand-letter the drawings, a very important subject in those days prior to computer drafting. Having studied and practiced architecture in Egypt, I had never hand-lettered any drawings in English before. Without giving me any prior warning, he embarrassed me by asking me to write notations on the blackboard. Of course, I did an awful job of writing. Prior to joining him in the classroom, I had no idea what he taught or what he wanted me to do, and he did not convene a meeting with me beforehand to explain what he needed done. I think he resented the fact that I was forced on him by the dean. After the class, he must have given Dean Taniguchi an awful report about my performance.

As a result of Oswaldo's complaint, the dean assigned me to another professor who taught freehand drawing. I was astonished at that professor's style of instruction. He jumped on a table and took strange poses after instructing the students to draw him without thinking about how the lines were formed, to convey the movements he was making. It was a unique method of freeing the students from the constraints of having to think about every line they put on paper. Our professors in Egypt would have never demeaned themselves by acting as a model in front of a class. I was assigned to critique the student's efforts and help in grading their drawings. That was an easy enough task.

Between TA assignments, I embarked on the research for the competition and before long found myself deeply interested in the work. I delved into catalogs of construction equipment used in the States and parallel systems such as container ship equipment and large cranes as well as other sources of information at the library about prefabricated housing systems. I researched the social implications of living in slums as well as the negative effects of urban renewal. In essence, I was my own best teacher. Based on that research I started sketching a machine I dubbed the "Slum Restructuring Machine," SRM for short. Inevitably, I would come to a dead end in the development of the SRM. Whenever I asked Professor Mather to help me find a solution, he would remind me that this was an individual effort and he could not give me any pointers. I had to evolve on my own and develop independent thinking. I believe this is the essence of higher education and realize Mr. Mather was right in letting me grope for solutions. After all, he was no expert on designing machines either.

The SRM is a large piece of equipment capable of lifting very heavy weights and hanging them above the existing slum area. Several of those machines would be towed to the slum in manageable component sizes, assembled and hydraulically expanded to their full size. They would be placed at predetermined locations to form a network whose function was to lift prefabricated apartment units. When those units were completed, the slum residents would be told to spend the day elsewhere while the existing slum was being bulldozed. The new apartments would then be lowered gingerly to rest on the existing foundations. Sometime later in the project, Professor Mather saw my sketches and said with a twinkle in his eyes, "When an Egyptian comes to Texas, he thinks really big," referring to how Texas is known for big things.

The Slum Restructuring Machine

Chapter 2
I MEET SOMEONE SPECIAL

The UT campus, like most major university campuses, is inviting, solidly built and with a well-organized layout. It had a lot of attractive female students but I had no way of getting to meet any of them. Since I had never dated in Egypt, I was rather awkward and shy, and had no idea how to start a conversation. My command of the language was not as developed as I would have liked it to be, especially since the language of American college students in the late sixties had evolved very differently from what I had learned from magazines and in school. My learning had been more formal and, of course, the kids had their own jargon which escaped me from time to time. This was also at the height of the hippie movement, so many words took on entirely different meanings. The students also had a weird sense of humor. For example, I read the following scribble on one of the toilet stall partitions: "Eat sh--, 500 billion flies cannot be wrong!" I guess whoever wrote it was trying to convey that one should not follow the herd mentality.

Foreign aid
About three months after I arrived in Austin, my brother Sobhi in Egypt, to whom I had granted power of attorney to act on my behalf there, contacted an accountant classmate of his to ask how he could get my remaining money out of the country. His friend had a client in Lebanon who had dealings abroad, requiring money transfers to conduct business. Unlike Egypt, Lebanon did not place restrictions on the transfer of hard

currency outside the country. My savings, which I had to leave in Egypt since I was allowed to take only the equivalent of $200 out of the country, were paid to that client and he transferred an equivalent amount, the kingly sum of $1800, to an account I opened in a bank in Austin. I had written that money off as the price of obtaining my freedom. As a result, I became lousy rich overnight! God works in mysterious ways.

The first thing I did after I received the money was buy a used 1962 Chevy II from a Thai graduate student acquaintance of mine for $500. To sweeten the deal, he convinced one of his friends, a student from Hong Kong, to teach me how to drive it. It was extremely hazardous duty for that poor guy, but we both survived. In spite of the fact that it was now 1969, which meant the car was seven years old and had probably belonged to several people before I bought it, it had only one problem, the gear shift would become stuck occasionally after a full stop. The seller told me about it and explained that if I raised the hood and pulled a certain linkage, the problem would be fixed. I followed his instructions and tried it the first time it acted up, and it worked. From then on, if the car didn't move at a stop sign or when the signal light turned green after a full stop, I jumped out, raised the hood, pulled the linkage, slammed the hood, jumped back in and went on my way. I am sure those behind me who witnessed this dance must have been either amused or maddened, but they did not honk their horns or cuss me. In a bigger city like New York or Cairo, it would have been a different story. I did not drive in Egypt because very few people had enough money to buy a car, and public transportation was used by all.

Car trouble
After Robert, the student from Hong Kong (most students who came from that city adopted English names to facilitate

communications, a smart move), discontinued the driving lessons to save his life and attend to his studies, I received four moving violation tickets in quick succession. The first was caused by the fact I was unfamiliar with stop signs (only stop signals or no signals at all were used in Cairo). I did not stop and broadsided another car. I admitted to the driver I was at fault and apologized, but he gave me a piece of his mind and called the cops. The officer was polite. He talked to each party independently about how the accident had occurred, and when I admitted I was in the wrong, he wrote me a ticket.

I got the second ticket just before Christmas. It cited my failure to turn on my headlights at dusk. I was told later by a friend that it should have been a warning ticket since one could see clearly in the well-lit streets of downtown Austin. However, cops were strict with college students, especially if they were foreign. I suppose that is as it should be, since many of them, like myself, were permitted to drive using an international permit which, I believe, exempted them from having to take a driving test (I don't recall whether I had taken the test before I started driving). Most foreigners are not as familiar with US traffic signage and regulations as local citizens.

The reason for the third ticket was driving five miles above the speed limit in an area where signs were rare and where the speed limit dropped abruptly at a bridge. I hadn't noticed the sign so I guess I deserved that one. The fourth was for changing lanes without activating my turn signal. Because there was little traffic at the time, I thought this too should have been a warning ticket. I had to pay a fine, which I could ill afford, for each of these tickets. However, at the time, the average fine was $5! After acquiring that record, I received a summons to appear before a judge to determine whether my driver's license would be suspended or even revoked. On the appointed date, I went to court. I was nervous as the judge reviewed my case. However, after quizzing me and the police officer about the incidents, he was gracious enough to dismiss the case provided I did not acquire another ticket during the course of a year. I was elated at the unexpected outcome and drove with extreme care and fear from then on. I have never been ticketed from that day to the present, thank God.

I change jobs

By the end of that semester, I was fed up with the Teaching Assistant (TA) job and needed a change to a position I could learn from. I continued to look at the bulletin board in The Commons (Student Union) and one day I saw an ad from the Architectural Engineering School asking for TAs to act as construction observers to monitor the progress of a federally financed, low-income housing project where several new building systems were being used. I applied and was interviewed by the professor in charge, who agreed to hire me. He invited me and a couple of other applicants to his house for beer and oysters and we had a pleasant, chatty evening. It was a nice change from my ham sandwiches. The job entailed writing notes listing the work being done every day, and taking many Polaroid pictures of each building to show the methods and materials used. I had to start at 8 o'clock in the morning. When I told the professor I was unfamiliar with the neighborhood and might get lost, he asked a student who lived near me to give me a ride to the job site. This worked out fine. He was a nice young man from Indiana.

Observing construction was interesting and educational. A rotating time-lapse camera mounted on a tower took bird's eye shots of the site. At the end of construction, the project manager gathered everybody in a conference room to watch the progress of the project as recorded by that camera. It was quite a show.

The still pictures were projected in quick succession which resembled a jerky motion picture showing all the building phases, from digging the foundation, to pouring the concrete slab, to framing and the work of the different trades until each house was built. I learned a lot from watching that job.

After the houses were nearing completion, we were notified an important visitor was coming to visit the site. Around 1 o'clock in the afternoon, a big black helicopter landed in a clearing on the site and I was amazed to see President Lyndon B. Johnson emerge. He was saluted smartly by the Marine officer and, surrounded by an entourage of photographers, toured the houses. I suppose that visit was a photo op. for his visit to the project which must have been part of his plan for "The Great Society." At the end of his tour, all the workers and the inspection staff, including me, lined up to meet the President. He started shaking hands and I, a newly-minted foreign student, got to shake the hand of the President of the United States. I still can't believe it.

New digs
After living in the rooming house for a year, the owner told me a larger and cheerier room had become vacant and "I would love it." He added that the rent would be $30. I couldn't have cared less about the cheerfulness of the room. It was just a place to lay down my head at night. However, I didn't want to rock the boat since I had already found a job and could afford the new rate. The old $20 room was equipped with what is called a swamp cooler, a kind of primitive window air-conditioning unit using water evaporation and a fan to cool the space. It had a fibrous filter made of excelsior, or thin shavings of soft wood, that was irresistible to squirrels. These critters used to tear parts of the filter at dawn, to use for nesting, I suppose. Of course, this startled me awake; not a great way to start the day

after working on the Slum Restructuring Machine project late the night before. Fortunately, the new room did not have that problem. It was cheerier because it had a larger window overlooking the street, but I still didn't have kitchen privileges and had to continue eating my cold ham sandwiches.

Dating

While looking at the want ads on the bulletin board at the Student Union one day during the summer session to find an alternative to my TA position, I saw an announcement for a first-of-its-kind computer-dating program introduced by students in the newly formed computer lab on campus. This was a part of a "Real Life" computer-programming experiment. It is amazing how God was looking out for me when I needed His help most. I immediately obtained and filled out one of the multi-page forms which required information about my age, ethnic background and a description of my appearance, height, weight, hair color, likes and dislikes, etc. I put it in an envelope along with a check for $5 and mailed it to the specified address. Ladies were allowed to participate for free. I was excited and waited impatiently for the response.

After a few days, I received a letter listing ten potential matches for dating along with their phone numbers. The letter also contained instructions about how to conduct the encounter, which were beneficial to me. It suggested that the first meeting be located at a public place like a café and that one should order a non-alcoholic beverage. Similar instructions were issued to the ladies. I was thrilled and, at the same time, apprehensive because of my inexperience. I also hated using the phone because it was difficult for me to understand what was said without seeing the lips and expression on the speaker's face. I later learned this is a common problem for newly arrived foreigners. It is amazing how much feedback one gets from watching expressions. Without this information, word meanings and nuances can be misconstrued.

With some trepidation, I finally picked up the phone and called the first name on the list. I identified myself to the girl who answered and explained that she was on my list of matches and asked whether she would meet me at Chambers (the only café I knew) at such-and-such time. I was pleasantly surprised when she agreed. I did this a couple of times with other girls, gaining a little more confidence each time. None of these encounters panned out for a second date because they were either too young or because there was no chemistry between us. On the fourth try, I waited for about five rings and then a girl with a sweet voice answered. After I introduced myself, the conversation went something like this:

"Hello."
"Are you Judy?"
"No, are you one of Judy's computers?"
"What?"

She laughed and explained that the girls in the dorm called the callers from the computer-dating program "computers"! It was the first time someone had called me "computer"! I got in the mood and said:

"Yes, I am."

We chatted a little because I didn't want to stop talking to such a cheerful person. She told me Judy was out but that she would take a message to give to her when she got back. I then surprised myself and before I knew it the next words were out of my mouth.

"How about you? Would you substitute for Judy?"
"I can't do that."
"Why not?"
"Because you are not on my list!"
"What difference does it make? You could still meet me."

She hesitated then said:

"I will, only if you promise to call Judy, but I have to warn you that I am short."
"Fine, I don't mind. I am not too tall myself. By the way, what is your name?"
"Gayle Hensley."

We agreed on a time and arranged to meet for a coke at Chambers (Just a few days afterward, Neil Armstrong landed on the moon). On the appointed day, I went to the café and waited a few minutes outside. Along came Gayle with a lop-sided smile and a limp. She was about 4'-11" tall, a bit short, as she said. At 5'-7", I felt tall; not an easy feeling to come by in Texas where it seemed that everybody was towering over me. We went inside, found a table and ordered our cokes then started talking about the weather. After exhausting that topic, she asked me where I was from and I asked what caused her injury. She told me she had polio when she was four years old. Our first impressions of each other were not as favorable as I visualized. I was hoping to meet a really stunning Marilyn Monroe-type girl to match her sweet voice. Instead, I was confronted by one who was less than perfect physically. She, however, had a nice demeanor and was easy to talk to.

After visiting for half an hour or so, I cudgeled my brain to find a way to end that awkward encounter without hurting her feelings. After a longish lull in the conversation, I asked, "Would you like to see the project I am working on at the School of Architecture?" It was something to allow me to make an exit. She enthusiastically agreed. I later discovered she also was trying to think of how she could make a graceful exit. She told me later how much she objected to my smoking and that she thought I was "haughty."

When we arrived at the graduate lab, I showed her the "Slum Restructuring Machine" and began to explain how it would work and what it would do to improve the terrible housing conditions in certain slum areas around the world. Gayle became interested as I started to explain the project and listened attentively with wonder in her eyes. Professor Swallow, one of the graduate advisers, was at the lab correcting papers. He listened with half an ear to what I was saying, looked at me and raised his eyes to the ceiling as if to say, "What are you explaining all that for?" Long afterward, Gayle told me I had changed into a totally different person during that explanation —articulate, witty, funny and interesting.

At the end of my presentation, I offered to escort her to her class, which was going to start soon. When we arrived, I asked, "Will I see you again?" Something only a foreigner would say. She was kind and did not say, "Let me think about it" or "I don't know" or "I don't think so." She said, "Sure." I got really brave and asked, "May I call you?" This, come to think of it, would have been what I should have said in the first place, if I had known any better. She said, "Yes." The way she talked was wonderful and I didn't want to lose this precious link to humanity in my drab existence. We engaged in many conversations after that which I will address later in the narrative.

I returned to the graduate lab and resumed work on the SRM.

In theory, the concept sounded great since existing streets would follow the same familiar routes with a few improvements, the tenants would not be dislocated to an area away from their jobs, friends and relatives, and the new units would be more modern and hygienic. Furthermore, through intelligent planning and increased density, open spaces would be created to introduce amenities that did not exist there before. Examples of new services included schools, clinics, farmers' markets, etc., to serve the community. However, I knew that the concept had several major flaws. Maneuvering such big machines may not be feasible in many, if not most, locations. One day to move the contents of the existing units, demolish the existing housing and lower the newly constructed apartments is not a realistic time frame for such an operation. The weight of the 4-story apartments would be impossible to hang, even from those gargantuan machines. Add to this the fact that this method would be too costly to execute since each machine would probably cost $50 million or more dollars. If we multiply that number by approximately ten machines, the initial cost of $500 million would be beyond the finances of many Third World country at that time. However, accomplishing all that thinking in two semesters and producing dramatic perspectives that caught the imagination on three large presentation boards impressed many of the people who saw it. It even surprised me.

I did finish the project and was astonished to learn the school had chosen it to be sent as the University's sole entry for the competition. I also found out the senior undergraduate class had been given the same assignment. While passing through one of the hallways, I noticed a display of projects related to that competition. One of them was interesting. It was, however, based on conventional thinking rather than my totally unorthodox and eye-catching project. I felt sorry when I saw the other student's disappointment at not being selected. If I had

had any influence in the matter, I would have decided to send it also. The school photographer took many pictures of my entry for the school record and enlarged them. To me, they looked even better than the original. A copy of the main perspective was framed and displayed in the School for several years afterward. That was highly gratifying for me. A student came to the graduate lab and asked me to write a description of the project to be included in the *Heliotrope*, a student publication. I wrote a detailed description and received a copy of the issue showing my project on the back cover.

After seeing my entry, one of the professors told me that it was sure to win an award. I told him that I wasn't so sure it would, since it was so fanciful and probably impractical. I was right; it did not win. However, there seemed to be another factor deciding the outcome of the competition. Most of the projects that won were entries from communist countries. The Soviet Union won four awards and Cuba had a single entry which also won an award. Whether it was by design or coincidental is anybody's guess. One must remember this competition was conducted during the height of the Cold War, and Argentina probably resented the hegemony of the United States. A few years after I became a registered architect, I entered the main perspective in a competition held by the Houston American Institute of Architects chapter and won a top-of-the-line Thermador microwave oven.

A few days after our first meeting, I called Gayle and enjoyed what was to become the beginning of many interesting chats. After that, I called her every evening and we talked about all the subjects that came to our minds, sometimes for as long as two hours. We played dictionary quiz—she would open her dictionary and choose the most difficult words she could find to see if I either knew the meaning or something related to it. Of course, I missed on a few occasions, much to her delight. One of the words that stumped me was kohlrabi, one of her mother's favorite vegetables which we didn't have in Egypt. As a result of those conversations, I did not feel lonely anymore and looked forward to our phone visits.

A long time afterward, Gayle told me it was a frustrating time for her because she could not understand why I did not ask her out when it appeared that I did like her and called her so often. She had no way of knowing I had no experience with dating since dating was not done in Egypt at the time I lived there. I had no idea what to do next. I was afraid if I did ask her for a date, she might think I was too forward and I would lose the only pleasurable experience I had up until then. In Egypt at that time, dating was serious business. One must be introduced by a relative to the family of the girl and ask the father's permission before being allowed to go on a date. An appropriate chaperone was assigned to accompany the couple and it was understood it was a prelude to a betrothal. I was not ready to make that kind of commitment, especially since I did not have a real job and could hardly afford the extra expense of dating.

At the end of the summer semester, during one of our long phone conversations, Gayle told me she was going home to her family until the fall semester started three weeks later. She said when she returned she would be at Andrews dorm, a different one from where she was living during the summer semester. I asked how I could contact her when she returned. She said since she was moving back to her previous room for the fall semester, she would have her old phone number and gave it to me. The three-week interval felt like an eternity. Finally the day she said she would be back arrived, and I called. Fortunately, she answered and told me that she had just entered her dorm room. I was delighted to hear her voice again.

It was a Sunday and the dorms did not serve an evening meal, so I invited her to share dinner with me at Church's Fried Chicken, a local fast-food chain near campus. It was all I could afford: $0.49 for two pieces of chicken and a roll each. I was glad she accepted and we had a delicious meal we both enjoyed. It was a nice change from the ham sandwiches that had become such a boring staple of my daily diet. We talked about her trip to her parents and I enjoyed her bubbly enthusiasm after that long interval during which my tongue had cleaved to my palate. And when I took her back to the dorm, I actually got up the nerve to kiss her goodnight! Wow! It was such a thrill the first time I mustered the courage to hold her dear face in my hands and touch her sweet lips. At 38 years of age, it was the first kiss I ever had. After that, we went on many enjoyable walking dates, met after my evening class for a soda and even went on grocery shopping outings to buy the ham sandwich ingredients for my daily meals.

On one of those walking dates, we passed by a hedge and, on the spur of the moment, I plucked a leaf and presented it ceremoniously to her saying, "This is a token of my green affection." I was amazed to find this simple gesture affected her deeply and made her eyes water with joy. I later found out she had kept that little leaf until it dried up and crumbled into dust!

We went on several dinner dates and sometimes ordered a pitcher of beer and a pizza, followed by a movie. After each date, I drove her to the dorm and we kissed at the door. I enjoyed those dates tremendously and she did too. It was the first time in my life I felt truly happy. On one of those dates, my car did its trick at a stop sign. Gayle got alarmed and worried about what we were going to do. I jumped out, raised the hood and, with my seemingly superior mechanical know-how, yanked the stuck linkage, closed the hood and off we went. She was duly impressed until I told her how the former owner had filled me in on how to solve that quirk. I was always honest with her, and she appreciated that. She always answered my questions, no matter how embarrassing they might have been to her, as forthrightly as possible. I didn't know a lot about women and their feelings, as well as about many things in the American culture. She later said she had a wonderful time sharing what she knew about all the subjects I asked about.

On another date we went to Zilker Park, a popular dating spot. It had rained the night before and the ground was wet. After we finished kissing and necking to our hearts' content, we were ready to leave. In the dark, I hadn't noticed that we were parked in a mud patch. I started the car and pressed the gas pedal but the wheels just spun and the car wouldn't budge. The more I pressed the pedal, the deeper the tires dug into the mud. I was beginning to wonder how we were ever going to get out of that fix when Gayle, who had more experience driving cars, suggested I rock the car by driving forward and backward in succession to pry the car loose from the mud. Thank God, this did the trick. I had a vision of being stuck there forever and having to explain why we were bogged down in that spot when they finally found us.

One day Gayle asked me whether I would like to meet her parents Thomas (Tommy) and Jurline Hensley who were visiting from Cuero. An alarm bell rang in my subconscious. In Egypt, if a girl asked that question of a guy, it was usually to snare him into making a commitment. I did not realize that in the States it was only to familiarize her folks with the fellow she was talking so much about, to satisfy their curiosity. She was astonished and hurt when I refused. When she asked for the reason, I told her I was not ready to make any sort of commitment at that time. She explained they were coming for a relative's wedding in Austin and that a meeting had nothing to do with commitment of any kind. With that reassurance, I assented. She is a very patient and uncommonly perceptive woman. When I met them, I was struck by her father's composure and dignity, and her mother did not seem like a potentially mean mother-in-law type, a common trait in some countries, especially Egypt. Not long after, Gayle graduated and was offered a teaching job in a small town called Edna, which is about 130 miles southeast of Austin.

Gayle's new job

Gayle needed a car in order to accept the job offer. After considering several models, she settled for a new VW Bug, because it was the least expensive car she could find. She chose one that had neither a radio nor an air-conditioner. She even asked the dealer to remove the white-wall tires to reduce the price by $5 per tire. The car came to approximately $1900. Today, you can't even buy a used golf cart for that amount. She paid half the price from her savings and her father gave her an interest-free loan for the other half, with the understanding it would be paid back in monthly installments. She was diligent in making the monthly payments while living frugally. Her yearly salary was about $8000, paid monthly, so she had to budget well. Her mother accompanied her during the search for a place to live. They found a tiny house to rent which had once been the gardener's quarters on an estate only a few blocks from the school. Gayle taught 6th grade. Her landlady, who lived in the main house, treated her like a granddaughter, sharing her garage so Gayle could protect her precious new car. She left the outside lights on when Gayle had a late meeting at school, and she often invited her to share a meal or to watch the evening news. Gayle could not afford a TV or even a radio, so this was a real treat. Her rent was only $40 a month including utilities! That landlady was a Good Samaritan.

We continued to see each other most weekends. She would get into that Bug of hers and race north at 80 miles per hour to meet me. Or I would head south to Edna for the day. Because of her teaching position in that very small town, we had to monitor where we went, even to what movie we might be seen attending. Gossip spreads rapidly and we did not want to risk her reputation. Sometimes we would meet at her parents' house for the day so they could get to know me better as well. Those were enjoyable days. I never did call Judy, the girl that Gayle had been answering the phone for and with whom I had been matched by the computer.

Being accepted at the University of Texas and not in a university located somewhere in the frozen north showed me that the good Lord was watching out for me. I loved the university, the friendly people of Texas, the assistance I received from Dean Taniguchi, Mrs. King and countless others. I am very grateful to God for helping me find a perfect companion in the person of Gayle and the joy she introduced in my life. Who could have imagined that something called a computer-dating program would have been introduced at the exact time I was beginning to despair of ever finding my significant other? Sure, life threw many surprises and disappointments at me, but things sorted themselves out and worked for the best according to His plan.

Before the summer recess in 1970, Joe Stubblefield, a senior who was a teaching assistant, passed by my drafting table at the graduate lab and was impressed by my efforts on the competition project. He told me he had started working at an architectural firm in town and suggested I go with him for an interview with one of the partners. When I arrived, the partner reviewed samples of my work and asked what I expected to be paid. I told him what I was making at UT. After the interview, he hired me for the summer at the same low pay. I felt like I was on top of the world. I learned a lot during that period about construction drawings as they are done in the US, and how an architectural firm functions.

My nephew arrives

Not long after I landed the summer job, I received a letter from Samir (Sam), one of my sister Hilda's sons whom I helped raise, asking if I would sponsor him for immigration to the US. While I was not in a position to assume a burden on my very limited resources, I decided to help him because I knew how bad conditions in Egypt were. I filled out the necessary paperwork, which included a testimony from my summer job employer stating what my income was and that I was considered a permanent employee, and mailed the letter to him. With that documentation, he was able to wade through the quagmire of government and embassy red tape. In the meantime, I decided I would need more than just a room for the two of us to live in and began to look for an apartment. I found a nice furnished studio apartment not too far from the rooming house, made the deposit and moved my few belongings there. Before I knew it, Sam sent a letter with his arrival date and flight number. I picked him up at the airport and drove him to my apartment.

I told Gayle about his arrival and she asked if she could come to meet him after he was settled. We set a time and Sam and I decided to invite her to dinner. Sam, who loves good food and thinks of himself as a grand chef, told me he knew how to fix a delicious meat dish. I drove him to the grocery store and he chose a thick slab of chuck roast, a bag of frozen peas and a roll of foil. He put the meat in the foil, added some butter, onion, pepper and the frozen peas around it. Then he wrapped the foil around everything, sealed it on top, and put it in a pan in the oven at 350 degrees for one hour.

We set the table and when Gayle arrived, he removed the pan ceremoniously from the oven and placed it on the table. The smell was wonderful. When we dug into the meat, however, it was on the tough side and most of it was a bit less cooked than even rare! Gayle, who was accustomed to her mother's delicious, tender roast, was diplomatic, watching how enthusiastic Sam was about his "masterpiece." She asked for the thinnest section, chewed heroically and said how wonderful it was. Personally, I was hungry and the taste wasn't too bad and I did not mind the meat's toughness too much. It contrasted favorably with my usual ham sandwiches. Finally, the meal came to an end and we left him in the apartment to go on our date. I did not have a TV to distract him and I am sure that he was afraid to leave lest he get lost. I felt sorry for him but it couldn't be helped.

Living together was an adjustment for both Sam and me, but we managed. Once he got his bearings, he started looking for a job. Since he did not have his driver's license yet, I drove him to job interviews. On one occasion, while we were stopped at a stop sign near campus, a couple of pretty coeds passed by and he smiled at them admiringly. Unfortunately, the one that was the object of his admiration gave him the finger, an internationally understood sign. It hurt his feelings tremendously. He couldn't imagine such a pretty girl could be so crude and unladylike. Social turmoil in the early1970s changed the outlook and mores for many young people, and it was at this time that Sam arrived. During the Vietnam era, there was intense fighting, the draft was sweeping up all eligible young men, including new immigrants with limited language skills, and within a few months there was a possibility Sam would be drafted into the military to fight in Nam, so I arranged for him to apply to join the National Guard and helped him find a job in his field through the want ads in the paper. He had graduated as an engineer in Egypt and was on his way to independence.

I propose
I was beginning to realize that life without Gayle would be meaningless and it was time to propose. I told my nephew that, since he had found a job, he could afford to rent a place of his own. I helped him find a studio apartment and he moved his few belongings there. Over the Thanksgiving holiday, about two years after we met, I asked Gayle to marry me and, because I could not afford an engagement ring at that time, gave her a gold bracelet I had brought with me from Egypt to sell in the US if I ran out of money. She responded to my proposal by saying, "Well….I don't know, I will have to think about it" I guess the question was kind of sudden without any romantic preliminaries like kneeling on one knee and surprising her with a disguised package. Her response, however, hurt my feelings since I did not pop the question until I was sure I loved her and that she loved me, and whenever we were apart we missed each other greatly. I persevered and she finally said yes before the weekend was over.

Being from a traditional family, Gayle explained that even though she had said yes, I would still have to ask her father for her hand first. This was a tough proviso but I agreed. However, no time was set for that event. Each time we went shopping, Gayle would look longingly at engagement rings in the windows of the jewelry stores. My question was always, "Wouldn't you really rather buy a refrigerator?" This was partly because I could not afford a ring and partly because I saw no value in something that was not truly useful. However, recognizing how important that issue was to her, I secretly went to Zale's jewelry store and applied for my very first loan, to buy a ring set, just before Christmas, as a surprise. That was the first time I had ever borrowed in my life and I didn't feel good about it.

Chapter 3
WE GET MARRIED

In 1970 Gayle and I arranged to meet at her parent's house on Christmas Day for gift-opening and dinner. They invited Sam as well. It was his first Christmas in the U.S. When I got to Cuero, the town where Gayle was born, I felt awkward and nervous. When Sam and I arrived, I sang out, "We wish you a Merry Christmas and a Happy New Year." We all gathered around the tree and handed out the gifts. Everyone opened one in turn. At last Gayle came to the one I had wrapped for her. She opened one box to find a smaller one inside. She opened ever-smaller boxes until she came to the ring box. At that moment, fearing that they would all see the ring before I asked her father for his approval, I shot up from my seat and blurted to her father, "I would like to ask you for your daughter's hand in marriage." My sudden outburst took everybody's breath away. I felt like an awkward fool, which was a pretty accurate description of my behavior. Her stunned father did not respond for a couple of seconds that felt like an eternity. I wouldn't have been surprised if he had refused after such a performance, but he recovered after looking at Gayle's mother and gave his blessing.

Gayle's dad
Gayle's father, Tommy, was a serious, hard-working man with a sense of humor. He was drafted into the Army Air Corps during WWII and saw action in the Pacific. Like many WWII veterans, he never said a word about his war experiences, which must have been horrific. When he returned to the US, he worked at several jobs, including as a butcher at a grocery store where he

met Gayle's mother. He later worked as a police dispatcher at the county jail during the night shift. Although of limited means, he did not hesitate to render assistance wherever it was needed. He opened a home business to sharpen knives, scissors, handsaws as well as chain saws. Because his was a unique service and he charged modest fees, people from the surrounding small towns and communities brought him their items to sharpen. His small shop, a non-air-conditioned metal building, was extremely hot, but that did not stop him, even in the worst south central Texas summers.

While Gayle was growing up, her mother, Jurlyne, took care of the home front. To help out with the finances as well as to help her qualify for Social Security later, she took in ironing and worked long hours at home. By working at home, she was also always there for Gayle and her younger brother. As was tradition at the time, Tommy took care of all money matters. Jurlyne is now 90 years old.

I get a job
After I finished my course work at UT, I applied at Brooks, Barr, Graeber & White (BBG&W), a sizable architectural firm in Austin. The interview with David Graeber went well and he said he would like Bill Paschal, a senior associate, to see my portfolio to decide whether he could use my abilities on a major hospital project he was entrusted with. That interview also went well and when he asked me what salary I expected, I said that I was making $2.50 an hour at my summer job. He offered me $4.50 an hour. I couldn't believe they would offer me more than the sum I mentioned. Thinking about this much later, I realized the salary must have been the minimum for an entry-level draftsman in that firm. It probably was well below what they would have offered a person with my experience and qualifications. It never occurred to me that that may have been

the case, as I was grateful for the opportunity and ready to do my best at the firm.

Now that I had a job, I decided to see whether there were any apartments that were better and larger than the one I lived in and would be suitable for Gayle and I when we got married. I was anticipating the fast-approaching time when the lease would come up for renewal. I visited several apartment buildings advertised in the paper and settled on one that was farther away from campus but was less noisy, better designed and had an inner court with a swimming pool. To me, it looked downright luxurious. The apartment was a furnished one-bedroom ground floor unit. Next, I looked at car ads in the papers and was impressed with the sharp-looking Opel 4-door hatchback. One weekend, I went to Covert Buick/Opel dealership and a salesman showed me a shiny red model with black interior. It was irresistible compared to the dated and much used Chevy II with its linkage problem. I asked about the price and he showed me the sticker. I had no idea that I was supposed to haggle and assumed sticker represented a fixed price. This is one of the disadvantages of being a naïve foreigner. He allowed me $200 for my car and I paid full price for the Opel. I accepted dealership financing and drove off rejoicing. It was a spiffy, powerful car and I was as proud as a king.

Having acquired a job, an apartment and a car, we were ready to embark on our wedding preparations. We set a date in June for the ceremony, I acquired a week's vacation from work and, at the appointed time, my nephew and I headed for Cuero. When we arrived, I discovered I had left my tie at home. Nelson, Gayle's younger brother, loaned me his. He rushed a couple of miles home to get another for himself. Since he was the acolyte, the service could not start until he returned to light the candles.

I felt rather embarrassed, but these things make a wedding memorable. Thankfully, the service was delayed only a matter of a few minutes and no one even noticed. The ceremony was a simple affair attended by a few people from the immediate family. My best man was Ronnie Kruhl and his wife, Carol stood up for us. He was an acquaintance from the Architectural Engineering School.

Our wedding

After the ceremony, we found the car decorated with the usual funny words and an assortment of cans tied to the back bumper. The wedding reception was at Gayle's aunt's home where we cut the cake, had punch and finger sandwiches and I met more of her family who had come for the celebration. I introduced Sam, who held his own and even seemed to enjoy the event. Afterward, Gayle and I drove back to our new apartment in Austin for our first night as husband and wife. I was now a married man!

Gayle's background

Gayle was born in Cuero, a south central Texas town of about 6500. Its name is Spanish for rawhide or leather. In the late 1800s it had been a way station for cowboys bringing cattle from the south to be loaded on trains and shipped north. Upon getting paid, those cowboys let loose with their money in the saloons as well as in the sizable red-light district common in towns along the cattle trails. Legend has it that cowboys would hide their guns in an old well behind one saloon when they heard the sheriff was on his way.

Gayle, Nelson, Jurlyne and Tommy

Gayle's handicap

Gayle was infected with the polio virus during the epidemic of 1952 when she was 4 years old. She was transported by ambulance to San Antonio. It was the closest city with a general hospital (Robert B. Green Hospital) equipped to treat victims of that epidemic. During the 85 mile trip, she stopped breathing twice and was resuscitated both times before reaching the closest general hospital equipped to treat polio victims in south central Texas. The doctors placed her in an iron-lung machine to help her breathe. The machine did the breathing for her by changing the air pressure inside. The nurses were nice to her and clipped a comic book to the machine to occupy her mind and prevent her from dwelling on her condition. She told me she would get frustrated when she reached the end of the page and nobody was there to turn it for her. Eventually she was weaned from the machine and she began to breathe on her own.

After she left the hospital, she went to Gonzales Warm Springs where she endured a lot of agonizing physical therapy and wore full-length metal braces on her affected leg and used crutches. Later on, she had surgery to implant staples in her left knee to slow the growth in the undamaged leg so there would be less difference in the length of her legs as she grew. Another operation was done in two phases to fuse her left ankle joint to keep the foot with the atrophied muscles from flopping and preventing her from walking. After healing from these two surgeries, she was able to walk without the heavy metal brace she had worn on that leg. Her indomitable spirit enabled her to rise above her handicap.

She hasn't lost that spirit in spite of the fact she is now suffering from Post-Polio Syndrome which causes a re-weakening of the nerves in the areas originally affected. This diagnosis came after she started to fall frequently and experience unusual fatigue at the end of the day. I suggested we get a wheelchair so we could continue doing the things we enjoyed without her becoming so exhausted that she could not continue. To me this was an obvious solution. I was surprised at her very emotional reaction. Only after we did get the wheelchair and found how much easier it made our travels, did she explain that using the chair symbolized a loss of independence to her that she had fought so hard to regain during rehabilitation. As her situation continues to deteriorate, she still finds it hard to accept the need for assistive devices. However, as it became harder and more tiring for me to push her, I looked into getting a scooter for her. I identified a small lightweight one she could use for traveling. This also meant changing from our beloved bright yellow sports wagon, which we called "Zoomie", to a mini-van that could be equipped with a scooter lift.

My research led me to a van in which the scooter could be installed over the fold-down third row seats. The scooter gave Gayle a new enthusiasm for life. She now zips around the grocery store and mall with ease and has a lot of fun at the same time. Since she can "out run" me, I had to find a way to keep up with her. Searching through the handicapped equipment catalogs, I found a companion chair (a wheelchair with 4 small wheels which requires a companion to push it) on the Internet. I now sit on the chair and grab a special belt attached to the scooter and she pulls me! We have explored Chicago, Seattle, Washington, D.C. and Disney World that way. People laugh, give us the thumbs up and ask if they too can hitch a ride. Many who are dragging after a long day of walking look at us with envy, saying we have come up with the ideal way to travel. I believe we have!

Honeymoon

The morning after the wedding, we packed the car to embark on our honeymoon. I told Gayle I was determined to take her out of Texas since she had never left the state. I had seen pictures showing the marvelous Carlsbad Caverns in New Mexico and thought it would be a good destination. On the way, we came across a ramshackle one-story building with a sign that declared it to be a museum. It was dusty and looked awful but the admittance fee was twenty-five cents so we decided to explore it. We discovered laughable displays of "fossils" and old-timey "artifacts" in dusty cases. After about ten minutes of roaming through the run-down building we went on our way and wondered how the people there had the nerve to call this a museum. To this day, we still chuckle over this "museum" when we drive through a small town with a building carrying that lofty label.

We continued on to Carlsbad Caverns and arrived in the evening. The trip took about seven hours at an average speed of 75 mph! I had no idea Texas was that huge. It was a grueling experience that took all the energy we had, and we collapsed into bed after we ate at a fast-food restaurant. In the morning, we visited the caverns, which were awe-inspiring. We proceeded downhill for what felt like miles and miles and saw how fantastic these caverns were. By the time we reached the bottom, our feet were sore and throbbing. Our calf muscles ached from walking down the sloping trail. We had lunch at the bottom cafeteria. Mercifully, there was an elevator to take us back up. We spent the next day recovering. We were supposed to continue the trip, but all we could think of was going home. It never occurred to me that that destination may not have been the best one for a honeymoon, especially for a person with a limp, but I did manage to get Gayle out of Texas!

On the way home from the caverns, we stopped at Palo Duro Canyon in the Texas panhandle. It was strewn with sun-dried wood, probably from mesquite trees. I selected a beautiful gnarled piece that we called our "honeymoon wood." It looked like a piece of sculpture. We still have it on the mantelpiece in the living room. It has survived all our many moves with very little damage. When I returned to work the following week, the office staff, including the partners, surprised me with a post-wedding party, served cake and presented me with a card. I wasn't accustomed to being the center of attention and felt awkward in the presence of the big bosses. The cake was delicious and the card had many funny captions, which Gayle enjoyed when I showed it to her later.

After we settled into the apartment, we discovered that we could reduce our rent if we replaced the landlord-provided furniture piece by piece. This would help improve our finances. We began looking for a sofa and found they were either very expensive or too soft or not the right dimensions for our comfort. We started with the sofa because it was the furniture piece the landlord charged the most for. Much to Gayle's disbelief, I told her I was going to make one! I spent several lunchtime hours drawing it at the office until I figured out how to make it work to the last detail. The final design was for a sofa that transformed easily into a twin bed. I determined the size and length of the redwood boards I needed (at that time, redwood was cheaper than hardwood) and bought a handsaw, some bolts, a hand drill and bits, and rubber webbing to use for the sofa back and seat support.

After several weeks working right in the living room of our small apartment, I was ready for the cushions. I bought foam rubber mattress material and cut it to the required size. Gayle volunteered to sew the dark green chenille fabric we bought, as I applied linseed oil to the boards that formed the frame. While Gayle was at her job on the weekend, I decided to sew the last cushion. When she returned she was pleasantly surprised and thankful I could do that and was glad that she didn't have to. After it was finished, we tested it and we both loved the comfort and simple look. The price was just right. That sofa proved to be a wonderful addition, providing us not only with great seating, but an easily converted guest bed that was used for a long time. We finally sold it many years later.

Our trips

During our early married life, we spent our vacations exploring the US. We would drive north to points of interest such as Yellowstone National Park where we saw grizzly bears and Old Faithful. We also went to Wyoming and saw the magnificent Grand Tetons. We took a raft tour down the Snake River and were delighted to see bald eagles and a moose for the first time. It also had a stretch of rapids that made it seem like a true adventure. Then, by chance, during our drive to Jackson Hole, we saw a sign that read "5-Minute Rides for $5" in front of a helicopter preparing to take off. We jumped at the chance and took a spin that was exciting and seemed to last much longer than 5 minutes. It was our first ride in a helicopter, an unexpected treat.

Every time we went on one of our vacation driving trips, we packed a big cooler with lunch items and stopped for meals at roadside parks. Many times we met interesting people. At one stop, we met a couple returning from a fishing trip. They gave us several smoked fish which we enjoyed thoroughly. We also took a small charcoal grill with us. In the evenings, when we stopped at a motel for the night, we would put chicken on the grill to cook while we swam in the pool until it was cooked. We loved those impromptu outings which needed no reservations or worry. The US was less crowded at that time.

On another occasion, we drove to Phoenix, Arizona, and spent a couple of days with an Egyptian school friend of mine from my undergraduate days. We enjoyed meeting his wife, whom he married before leaving Egypt. Of course, the heat was oppressive but we did see the Petrified Forest. After leaving

Phoenix, we went north toward Utah and saw dinosaur tracks at a museum. We also visited the Grand Canyon. Gayle walked to the rim and said, "I can't believe what I am seeing, this is so awesome." It was truly magnificent. We also visited Colorado and shared a car tour with another couple to the top of Pikes Peak. During that trip, we learned its elevation is more than 14000' and it was discovered by Zebulon Pike, an explorer in 1806. It was a harrowing ride on a gravel road with many sharp curves and drop-offs that seemed only inches away. We saw chipmunks for the first time. They were almost tame and came right up to us. I was totally impressed by the variety of landscapes, the friendliness of the people and the size of this wonderful country.

We buy a house
After about a year of living in the apartment, I heard chit-chat among my co-workers indicating many owned their own homes instead of renting. This started me thinking, "Why not us?" I looked into the pros and cons and found no reason for delay. After searching in the real estate section of the paper, I found a new three-bedroom house with two baths and a two-car garage for $19,560 (this was 1971 and home prices were still reasonable) in a neighborhood off Rundberg Lane, which used to be in far north Austin (today it is considered to be close to the city core but unfortunately, it has deteriorated into a depressed and unsafe area). The mortgage payment was well within our means.

When I made the suggestion to Gayle that we look at the house and seriously consider buying it, instead of the excitement I had experienced at the prospect of moving to a new house of our own she became so upset, her eyes teared up. "We can't afford to do that. Are you trying to make us go bankrupt? Where are we going to get that kind of money?" I wrote down how much it was costing us to rent the apartment and how much the mortgage payment for the new house would be. I also estimated the tax advantage and factored in the added cost of utilities. I stated that while the rent was money going down the drain, a mortgage payment would be building equity toward a better sale price. The figures showed the difference to be approximately $10 a month more than we were paying for rent. I explained that this move would also benefit us since the house would increase in value over time.

Our first home

Gayle, being a smart woman, could not believe her eyes and said, "If this is the case, let's go for it." To explain her hesitation and alarm, she told me later her parents had endured living through the Depression and did not believe in going into debt or buying anything on credit. Consequently, her reasoning followed their philosophy, which mandated that if a person couldn't buy an item for cash, he or she could not afford it. In retrospect, their approach is a good one, considering how the economy can plummet and falling home prices can demolish people's finances. However, in this case, I thought we were making a safe bet.

Gayle has always acted responsibly. One example was she had paid off the remainder of her car loan to her father before we got married. She wanted to start that phase of her life with a clean slate. I realized how lucky I was to have married a frugal, responsible woman who was not obsessed with shopping for shopping's sake. I don't think many women in this day and age are like that, and I continue to thank God for linking my fate to hers. After all, I also came from a family that did not have money to spare, and I have lived frugally all my life.

Getting the mortgage, however, was not easy since we did not have a credit record. I discussed that problem with the office accountant. He told me not to worry, saying his wife was an officer in one of the banks and he would put in a good word for me. I hardly knew the guy. People's good will never ceased to amaze me. This would never have happened in Egypt. Gayle and I went to the bank, signed an awful lot of papers and were approved for the loan. We then went to the realtor and signed another extensive batch of papers and became owners of our first house. It was a really exciting day.

The first day after we moved our few possessions in, I went to open the sliding glass door leading to the side yard and stopped abruptly when I saw a Black Widow spider with its young nesting in the track of the door. I hurriedly squashed them. It was one of those surprises that one can find in Texas. I was glad I knew how dangerous that kind of spider could be, having once spiders, I always hated them but I am sure she would have approved of what I had done.

Austin was a pleasant city with a population of approximately 250,000 when I was enrolled at UT. Its people were very friendly and still are to this day. I would walk down the street and a stranger coming in the opposite direction would smile and say, "How are you?" or "Howdy." In contrast, Cairo's population was 4,000,000 people during my sojourn there. Unless you knew somebody, your existence would not be acknowledged. This was one reason that made me like Austin from the beginning, and it was a strong factor in the decision to later retire just north of that city. Another is that the weather was similar to what I experienced in Cairo, except for the brief ice storms during the winter. The mild weather was definitely a plus.

Chapter 4
NEW OPPORTUNITIES IN TEXAS

Early on, I realized that to have any status in an architectural office, one must pass the licensing exam to become a registered architect. Accordingly, I went to the state registration office to get information and any material associated with the application. The architect managing the office listened to my accent, took one look at me and asked whether I was a citizen. When I said I had a green card and would be eligible for citizenship in two years, he said with smug finality that foreigners were not allowed to take it and added, unnecessarily, "Anyway, no foreigner can ever pass the state licensing exam." He acted like any typical lazy bureaucrat and was relieved he didn't have to do anything. I took it in stride since I could do nothing about it and thought what an inconsiderate oaf he was.

Anyway, most candidates took the exam more than once before they were able to pass it. Waiting two years would not be a great setback. I suspect the requirement for citizenship was formulated to prevent foreigners from competing with Texas architects. Fortunately, one year later, the citizenship stipulation was rescinded since the exam was a test of ability and should not be tied to what nationality the candidate belonged to as long as he or she was a legal resident. I paid the fee and took the three-day exam and found parts of it rather difficult.

I was surprised when I received a letter several months later informing me I had indeed passed it the first time. I was elated and disappointed at the same time. Elated because I didn't have to pay the fee to take it again and I could tell the guys at the office that I passed it the first time. I was disappointed because there were parts of the test that I thought I needed to pursue to gain more proficiency. Now that I had passed, I had no incentive to make the extra effort. Some of the guys from the firm who took the exam with me did not pass. They had been the ones who were so sure they would pass it the first time. While everybody congratulated me, the firm did not give me any raise to reflect my achievement. I knew this registration would be useful if I had to apply for a new job. It also allowed me to use the title Architect, instead of just Draftsman.

Now that we could afford it, I told Gayle that I would like to send a package of items to my brother Sobhi in Egypt. She got enthusiastic and helped me choose useful items from the grocery store that were too expensive or not commonly available there, such as nice soaps, certain kinds of canned food, electric shavers, etc. She packaged them properly and we mailed them to Sobhi, telling him to distribute them to the family. We felt good about doing it and hoped the family would enjoy getting a few niceties. We did this about three or four times during that year. Every time, we received a nice thank-you note. The last time, however, he (Sobhi) sent us a letter begging us not to send any more packages. My brother explained that the people at the post office usually opened the package as a "security measure" to prevent contraband, arms or harmful materials from entering the country because Egypt was at war with Israel. They inspected the contents and estimated their value (actually they doubled or tripled their value) to assess taxes on the contents! This was standard procedure applied to all imports. He said the boxes containing the last two packages were torn apart, crudely taped back together and stamped "Damaged in Transit" and were delivered empty. As if that wasn't bad enough, before they handed him the package, Sobhi still had to pay the exorbitant tax. I thought I had seen how low thievery could sink when I lived there. I had no idea how evil their inventiveness could get until I received that message. Of course, we stopped sending packages.

About three years after I joined the staff at BBG&W, the firm was acquired by a major Houston firm. Mr. Barr, one of the partners, called me to his office and informed me that, due to lack of projects, they were letting me go. I was stunned. I had been working hard and everybody had expressed satisfaction with my work. I did not expect this. He was kind enough to say they liked my work and that he would give me a letter of recommendation to an associated firm in Dallas, as well as the name of the principle to contact. We had been in our new home only 18 months and I felt awful about having to tell Gayle about this layoff, but I gritted my teeth and broke the news as gently as I could. She was devastated, not only about the fact we had to move again, but also because she really liked working at St. David's Hospital, renting TVs to patients. I applied everywhere in Austin but nobody was hiring. Finally, after three months of idleness, I told Gayle I had decided to go to Dallas to interview with the architect Mr. Barr recommended. I called Dallas and arranged for an interview.

Dallas

Gayle and I drove to Dallas. At the appointed time, I met the project manager I was told about. The interview went well and he offered me the position. However, after considering it, I became concerned because that company was also owned by the same company from which had laid me off. I decided to apply to other companies in the area to see if I could find a better alternative. Another firm granted me an interview. I met with one of the partners and showed him my portfolio. He became interested and invited one of the project architects to review my work. We discussed salary and benefits, after which he told me he would discuss it with the other partner and call me the next morning.

I received the call the next day, after we returned to Austin. He said everything looked good and asked me to start in two weeks. Gayle and I went back to Dallas and rented an apartment not too far from the office and put our house in Austin on the market. We put most of our furniture in storage and took only what we would need to live in the apartment until our Austin home sold and we could look for another house. Eventually, the house sold without any loss to us.

I thought I had found a permanent job. It was only much later that I realized that in the field of architecture there is no such thing as permanence unless you are a partner. Whenever the economy hit a downward trend, firms let go a bunch of people and when the economic situation improved, they started hiring again. Most of the layoffs occurred around Christmas. A year later, the company I had first interviewed with was closed by the parent company, the same company that closed down the one in Austin, proving that my fears had been well-founded.

A new car
A couple of months after I started work at my new job, the top of the back seat of my Opel started to crack, either from the sun or from the breakdown of the vinyl material. Of course that happened a few weeks after the end of the warranty. I became so mad I decided to put it up for sale. Gayle tried to dissuade me but I was adamant. I just wanted to get rid of it before something else went wrong. The way I thought about it, I would lose some money and get a brand new American-made car instead of that foreign one, which I had felt guilty about buying

in the first place. I believed the "Mr. Goodwrench" hype and thought GM cars were better than any other cars on the road. Was I wrong!

I liked the design of the newly introduced (translation: unproven) Chevy Vega and bought a spanking new mustard-yellow hatchback after they reduced the price fractionally. I discovered almost immediately it was one of the worst cars manufactured by GM. The day we drove it off the dealership lot, the stick shift came out of its socket when I tried to shift at a signal light. It had to be towed back to the dealership. When we went to pick it up after a few days of repair, the motor died at the first stop sign and it again had to be towed back to the dealership. A couple of weeks later, we had to have it towed again to fix other problems. So instead of enjoying a new car, we were without it more than we had it to drive. In addition, it had the first aluminum engine block produced by that company, it leaked and had to be fed a quart of oil every week. Whenever we drove it, we were trailed by a cloud of white smoke. This vehicle was Gm hasty response to Toyota's success in introducing small cars in the US. We kept that car for about three years of constant suffering before we traded it in for a dependable Honda Civic.

When the Christmas season arrived, I went to Republic Bank to deposit my check during my lunch break. The interior was decorated and a pretty young lady was delivering a magnificent rendition of O Holy Night." She had a rich, vibrant voice and was obviously an opera singer. Her rendition made whatever hair was left on my head stand on end! I wished Gayle were with me to enjoy that fantastic performance. It surprised me such a heavenly sound would be located in a bank, an institution devoted to dealing in money instead of spirituality.

The new job

The new office assigned me to a team working on a junior college. I was to develop the plans based on the preliminary design. My work included figuring the dimensions. Unfortunately, I made a mistake because the building had a complex geometry. I scaled some of the dimensions instead of figuring them mathematically. That is what we used to do in Egypt, and I didn't realize that a small fraction of an inch would make a difference. A very wrong assumption! The project architect became incensed when the structural engineer pointed out the mistakes. This made him lose face because project architects put on this aura of infallibility. If I had been in his shoes, I would have spot-checked the dimensions before I sent them outside the office, especially since he was dealing with a new employee. As the saying goes, "Trust but verify."

He called me to the conference room and, raising his voice, expressed his wrath in a fashion that infuriated me. I reacted strongly to it. He backpedaled, knowing if I left at that point in the project, he would not be able to finish on time. I made the necessary corrections and conferred with him whenever I had the least doubt about anything. After that we had daily contact and treated each other with respect. He invited Gayle and I to dinner at his house, and I assumed that the situation had been resolved. However, after the project was finished, the office manager called me to his cubicle and told me with belligerence that my employment has been terminated and that I should clear my desk immediately. I quickly applied to another firm and was hired. I enjoyed working at that office much more; then, as usual, the firm ran out of work and I was laid off a year after I was hired.

Mumps

About three years after our wedding, we discussed starting a family. We were not sure what problems Gayle might have carrying a child so, during her next routine physical, she discussed it with her doctor. After some tests, the doctor told her there was no physical reason why she couldn't bear children. Because of her polio history, he told her she may have to use crutches during the last months of pregnancy in order to lessen the stress on her weak leg. As distasteful as it might be to me, I considered being tested to find out whether I had a problem because of my medical history. I had had all the childhood maladies such as measles, the flu, chicken pox, colds and the mumps. The common wisdom about mumps at the time was once you had the mumps, you became immune for life. In my early twenties, however, I had awakened one morning with mumps-like symptoms. I went to my doctor and, sure enough, I had the mumps...again. He told me at the time there was a chance that I would become sterile. When I asked him if that meant I would not be able to get married, he assured me that it would have no effect on my enjoying a normal sex life but there was a chance I would not be able to father children. After I remembered that, I realized perhaps we may not become parents and reconciled myself to that fact. After all, if Gayle did not have any problem with that situation, why should I?

A citizen, finally

During our time in Dallas, I became eligible to apply for citizenship. I filled out the paperwork and passed the test. The swearing-in ceremony took place in a large courtroom in 1973. Once everyone took the oath, we were each given a small American flag that I have to this day, as well as our naturalization certificates. At that time I had the choice of changing my name to simplify communications. I considered changing my first name to a similar-sounding western name like Floyd or Fred but Gayle was very much against it, saying my first name had been given to me by my parents at birth.

Later I did adopt Fred to use for business. This made phone conversations so much easier. Prior to using Fred as my first name, I used my given name, Fouad. When I made a business call, the conversation often went like this:

"Hello, my name is Fouad Nashed."
After a longish pause, the recipient said:
"What?"
I repeated my name slowly, enunciating the words.
"Can you spell that?"
"F-O-U-A-D N-A-S-H-E-D."
"Can you repeat that?"
After I repeated it a couple of times, the recipient would say:
"Can I help you?"

I guess he said that because he gave up or decided not to press the issue any longer and waste time. The conversation went downhill from there because he had decided my English was unintelligible (it wasn't, since I had no difficulty being understood at the office). It was rather disheartening. After I adopted the name Fred, I had no more difficulty.

A week after I was let go, I received a letter from Richard Swallow, the graduate adviser at the School of Architecture, stating that he was wondering what had become of me. He also said he tried to call me but found my Austin phone had been disconnected. His letter was marked with an "unknown address" stamp and was forwarded to my Dallas address by the post office. He also wrote that my five-year grace period for presenting my thesis was going to expire soon and informed me it would be a shame to abandon my quest for a Master's degree after completing all the course credits. He also said I could present my thesis by mailing segments of it to be reviewed and returned with their comments. (The requirement was that the finished thesis would take the form of a bound book). Professor Swallow's letter also stated he could grant me an additional six months beyond the deadline if I needed the extra time.

Gayle urged me to take that opportunity, so I said to myself, "What have I got to lose? I am between jobs and can devote full-time toward tying that loose end." Gayle said she would look for a job because she had become bored with staying at home all the time and would enjoy working again. That would generate enough income to help with expenses so I could work exclusively on the thesis in order to finish it quickly. She applied for a job in the accounting department at Best Products, a chain of catalog stores (now out of business) dealing with upscale products at discount prices. As usual, they were impressed by her personality and work record and hired her.

As a challenging subject for my thesis, I decided to explore how to make cities grow in a more orderly fashion. I chose the title "Organic Urban Growth." I called and thanked Professor Swallow and told him I would start immediately and gave him the subject of my research. He approved my choice and informed me that another professor from Germany would join in critiquing and judging my work and they were looking forward to working with me. Now I had a goal to strive toward an interesting subject to explore. The change of pace would be a nice diversion from the grind of working at an office and looking for jobs. Once again things fell into place according to God's plan.

I had a book about urban planning that I read from cover to cover and also went to the local library to research my subject. I spent hours reading and organizing my thoughts before handwriting my ideas and conclusions. Since I was never taught how to type, Gayle used her manual typewriter to type my notes and retype them when I made corrections or changes in her spare time. We soon realized she needed help with this huge task since the manuscript required footnotes at the bottom of the pages. This was a job for a professional. She engaged the services of a freelance typist who charged by the page to type the text. This was before the advent of word-processing and computers and the typist used an IBM Selectric typewriter. The typist had to retype every page that I amended, regardless of how few the changes were. We were thankful she charged very low rates. During that time, I did not want to be bothered with shaving and grew a beard. Gayle liked it very much and said I should keep it. It still adorns my face, and my mother-in-law comments negatively about it every time she sees me. This, of course, means I will always wear it! In due course, I finished the 90-page thesis which included a number of illustrations of original visionary ideas explaining how a city can use the kind of growth mechanisms found in nature, such as amoeba cell division, tree growth rings, and extended roots in plants. I then developed sketches showing how that methodology could be applied as solutions to the problems encountered by cities. I had it bound in book form and mailed two copies of the finished books to the university.

Of course, that final thesis occurred after much back-and-forth correspondence and my adoption of some of the suggestions from the reviewers. After the bound copy was reviewed and accepted in 1975, I received a copy of the book with a gilded stamp and my Master of Architecture degree. Thinking back about the time I spent in the Dallas/Fort Worth area, I am amazed at how God works in our lives. Every time I was faced with a door slamming in my face, the Lord opened another. I did learn a lot during that time and gained experience. I finished the thesis closing a loose end that was nagging at me through his intervention when he inspired Professor Swallow to contact me about my thesis rather than give up after he found out that my phone was disconnected. I consider myself fortunate to have had the opportunities that were given to me.

In Fort Worth
After I finished the thesis, I decided to explore firms in Fort Worth and was invited for an interview at Lawrence White & Associates. When I went there, I was interviewed by Mr. White and hired as a project designer. That was the kind of work I loved. I carpooled from Dallas to Ft. Worth, sharing the ride with two other employees. One was the firm's mechanical engineer and the other was the specifications writer. After learning I used to build models of war planes, the mechanical engineer regaled us with stories about flying his P-47 Thunderbolt during WWII.

I designed several buildings which were accepted by the clients without any modifications. Mr. White (we called him Larry) was pleased and paid the yearly fee to enroll me as a member of the American Institute of Architects. I was considered a valuable asset in the firm since I finished each assignment in a relatively short time and was on good terms with the vice president in charge of design, Jim Vickery.

On one occasion, Jim told me we would be flying to Texarkana to present the project I had just finished to the review committee at East Texas State University. He said we would go in the company plane. I had no idea the company of forty employees even had a plane. I gathered the drawings and we drove to a private airport and boarded a twin-engine Cessna piloted by Larry and co-piloted by Jim. I learned later that Larry had a heart condition and always flew with Jim as a backup. Both were veterans of the Korean War. We had to detour around cloud formations to avoid turbulence but made the trip safely and the meeting went well. I was not invited to say a single word, for which I was grateful. I was included just to answer any design questions that might be posed by the client. Fortunately, there were none, and the project was passed on to the construction drawing department.

A university building project in Texarkana

A year after my employment at that firm, Larry decided to hire an executive vice-president to take some of the load off his shoulders. That individual, whom I secretly nicknamed Igor because his behavior reminded me of a Russian Tsar, started wasting everybody's time by convening frequent, unnecessary meetings to stir up things to prove he was a wonderful addition to the firm and that he was in charge. He suggested I change everything that I designed just for the sake of asserting his authority. In my opinion, implementing his suggestions would have ruined the designs because his ideas were not based on sound design principles, technical considerations, cost or even aesthetics. Of course, if any problems occurred as a result of those changes, I would be held responsible.

I did not like Igor's approach. We had arguments which resulted in my being summoned to Larry's office. He told me he had hired him (Igor) to share the work load he was struggling with and asked me to be more patient and to humor him. I went along and did as I was told. Igor interpreted my new attitude to mean he could become even more assertive and rambunctious. We began to argue again, and I was reluctantly let go by Jim, the Vice President. I could see he was not convinced this was the right thing to do but had to do it to avoid creating waves.

Before the lay-off Gayle had talked about going to Egypt to visit my family since they had asked repeatedly when I would return to see them. We had heard about a charter flight from New York to Cairo, arranged through a Coptic church there which made the cost of our tickets affordable. Gayle became excited at the prospect of seeing a country she had heard so much about, an exotic, faraway country with camels and different customs. In actuality, I dreaded having to be subjected to the antagonism and bad manners of government bureaucrats again (I had waited till I had an American passport to lessen the chance of having problems with the Egyptian authorities) but I did not want to deprive Gayle of the thrill of exploring that faraway land of the "mysterious East" and the opportunity to meet the rest of my family. I knew she would like those I spoke often about, the places where I grew up as well as visit the past glories of Ancient Egypt.

We decided to go ahead with the trip since the airline ticket money was unrefundable. We flew to Cairo and spent time with my family, ate at their homes and bought some Ancient Egyptian plaques (plaster casts from temple walls) as mementos. We visited the Pyramids, and Gayle was awed by the scale of those gigantic monuments. While there, we rented two camels and Gayle mounted one and explored the area from atop that high animal. One of the surprises that tourists experience is that those animals are *barraked* (meaning, brought to a kneeling position), positioning the saddle at a level low enough to allow the rider to get on. Once mounted, the animal is commanded to raise itself up on its hind legs, which pitches the rider violently forward, then to unfold its front legs, pitching him or her backward. One had to hold on to keep from falling off during those maneuvers. I alerted Gayle to that fact but, unfortunately, her saddle horn was broken and she had to hold on to the camel's saddle for dear life. It was quite an experience. She did enjoy that unique ride and petted the camel afterward. Even now she gets excited at the sight of a camel in a movie or on TV.

Gayle's pet camel   **Holding on for dear life**

Cairo
In Cairo, Gayle met my family for the first time. They were able to converse with her because English is taught in Egyptian schools. We also visited the Egyptian Museum of Antiquities with its unique, world-famous artifacts. While the contents were incomparable, tourists had to use flashlights to see the details in the displays within the poorly lit, dust-covered cases. There was no interesting theme nor was it organized into dynasties so the various kingdoms would be distinguishable. It was like a warehouse filled with fabulous pieces grouped haphazardly together. We got tired of seeing whole galleries

showing the same thing. We walked quickly through one of them and I explained the displays as, "pot, pot, pot, etc." which made Gayle laugh. This was in the seventies, I have no idea what it is like today. They may have reorganized it or some looting may have occurred during the chaos of the uprising after the ouster of the deposed President Morsi of the Moslem Brotherhood.

My brother-in-law Ezzat had arranged for a travel agent who was his relative to determine an itinerary and select a local guide to assist us when we visited the temples in the south. On that trip, we took the train south to Luxor and went to the Winter Palace Hotel where Churchill stayed when he visited Egypt during the war. The first night, Gayle became sick and delirious. I became concerned and asked whether we should call a doctor. I am glad when she refused because, at that time, the quality of care there could be extremely hazardous to her health. In the morning, she felt a little better and, as the day progressed, she improved enough for us to continue our sightseeing.

Luxor

We visited the valleys of the Kings and Queens where we descended into the Tut-Ankh-Amun (King Tut) tomb and toured the temple of Queen Hatshepsut and the magnificent temples of Karnack (see cover) and Luxor. Gayle was impressed by the glories of the Ancient Egyptians. For our meal, our guide recommended a native restaurant and said that it looked bad from the outside but served good food. We took a horse-drawn carriage and, while I was helping Gayle descend, a small schoolgirl asked her companion incredulously, "Is he taking her (a foreign tourist) in there?" because tourists had never been seen there before. She assumed that I didn't speak Arabic. I turned and said, "Yes, I am" in Arabic. Their mouths fell agape in surprise and mortification, and they ran away giggling. Another time we were walking along the sidewalk and four teenage girls were behind us. They started talking about us in Arabic among themselves, wondering where we were from and where we were going. When there was a lull in their conversation, I turned and answered one of their questions in Arabic. They smiled sheepishly for having been caught. Gayle enjoyed that trip of a lifetime. I, on the other hand, endured it but shared her fun. When we landed back at LaGuardia Airport, I understood why some people want to kiss the ground when they return to their homeland (the US is my homeland now, thank God).

On to Houston

After I drew a blank when I looked for work in Dallas, I applied at several Fort Worth firms but there were no jobs there, either. I had heard that firms in Houston were busy, so I sent my résumé to a major firm and was invited for an interview. On the morning of the appointment Gayle and I left Dallas in our miniscule 1978 Honda Civic. During the night, the area had been hit by an ice storm and everything was coated with a thick layer of the slippery stuff. The freeway heading south was very slick and I was driving at about 25 to 30 miles per hour like everyone else. There were large and small trucks as well as cars littering the shoulders of the freeway. Big semi-tractor trailers looked as if they had been tossed off the road, several lying on their sides in the ditch.

All was going well until the semi-truck driver in front of us decided to change lanes to go around the one in front of him, presumably to avoid the chance of a collision. That maneuver caused his truck to start whipping back and forth until it slid off the highway. It did stay upright but he was stuck. As a result of the drama occurring in front of me, I was forced to touch lightly on the brakes. Our car started a sickening slow-motion skid toward the right side of the pavement. It was a harrowing experience because I could do nothing to change direction or slow down. We came to rest in the grassy area beyond the shoulder of the road. I tried to drive out, but the wheels just spun in place. Even rocking the car forward and back had no effect. I thought we would have to spend the rest of the day in the freezing car and I would miss my interview. This was before cell phones so my interviewer would think I had not shown up, not a good impression to make.

The truck driver who caused our situation must have seen what happened in his rear view mirror. He climbed out and slid across the freeway to our car. At the same time, another trucker from a stranded semi across the freeway literally skated over to us. After determining we were okay, they offered to get us back on the pavement. They told Gayle to get in the driver's seat and step on the gas slowly as the three of us went behind the car, pushed it and guided it to the road. I was totally impressed by their thoughtfulness, brawn and courtesy. We were on our way again and soon drove out of the icy area as we headed south.

I went for the interview, was offered the job and gladly accepted. I was relieved the crisis was over and we went back to Dallas to make arrangements for the move. We put our house on the market and returned to Houston to rent an apartment until we could once again find a house. We put most of our possessions into storage since this worked well in the past. All went as planned until I reported for work. My interviewer told me sheepishly that his boss decided that they did not need me after all. While that behavior was extremely unfair, I decided to move on and began the job search once again. I interviewed with Bernard Johnson, Inc., an engineering firm which had a sizable architectural department and was made an offer on the spot.

Model of the Bus Maintenance Facility

I was assigned to a team working on the design for a major bus maintenance facility project for the City of Houston. The facility was complex, with thirty maintenance bays, a major maintenance wing devoted to rebuilding engines and transmissions, a parts storage and dispensing department, and specialized shops for electric wire harnesses, electronic equipment, upholstery, etc. In addition, there was a management wing and an independent fueling and fare-collection building. The project manager was an electrical engineer instead of an architect, as is the case in an architectural firm. The project architect, who had a staff of four, had visited similar facilities around the country to see examples and take pictures, which were compiled into several albums. The programming and sketching had been going on for more than a year without any definitive design to show for that effort.

During that time the city acquired the privately owned and operated bus company. The new owner changed the building program and the project architect quit after coming up with a rudimentary schematic sketch. While other members of the team were assigned to draw the plans for small parts of the project, I was given the task of developing the overall plan for the facility. I worked on the design with enthusiasm, developing the very rough sketch drawn by the project architect and finishing the final Design Development Phase in record time, complete with interior and exterior perspectives. Everybody was impressed and I was walking on air. Because of the shape of the building, they referred to it as the "Starship Enterprise"!

Around the start of the project, Gayle shopped for a permanent residence and found a nice, modern, three-bedroom house with clerestory windows that was only 6 months old in a suburb southwest of downtown. We bought it and after closing the deal moved our few everyday belongings from the apartment. Soon after, we had our furniture delivered from storage. Weekends were spent making the house suitable for us. Because the neighborhood was new, only two out of the eight yards that made up our block had been fenced. As we met our neighbors, one of the top jobs on their to-do lists was to put in fencing. Together we hatched a plan to put wooden privacy fences around each house. We thought working together and buying all materials needed would help keep the costs down. I drew up a plan and estimated how many bags of cement and how many posts, rails and boards we would need. Then we went shopping. We had the materials delivered and put into the garages of several of our homes.

On the first weekend, we rented a big gas-powered posthole digger that took four men to operate. We dug all the holes in one day and returned the auger. Then each weekend, we worked on building the fences. The men did the heavy work, and the women served lots of juice, water and cold drinks. They prepared meals for everyone. While it was a lot of hard work, it enabled us all to save money and we became more than just passing acquaintances. In fact, Gayle and the woman who lived behind us became such kindred spirits that I installed hinges on one of the posts and a latch attached to the next panel so they could open that impromptu door to visit face-to-face as well as pass things back and forth. Many phone calls between the two arranged these "meet at the fence" get-togethers during the nine years we lived in that house. Gayle and I also constructed a wooden deck and trellis in the back, right off the kitchen. We dug the holes, mixed the concrete in a wheelbarrow and planted the foundation posts. We included a wraparound wooden bench, making it a great place to barbecue and sit. Gayle planted wisteria which covered the trellis in a relatively short time and improved the atmosphere in the backyard. Houston is plant-friendly because of the humidity and abundant rain. We enjoyed living there in air-conditioned comfort in spite of that humidity.

Soon after our move, Gayle found a part-time job with a company that installed sprinkler systems. Though she stayed for about six months, it did not offer her the opportunity to make friends since only one other woman worked there. At almost the same time she was deciding to start another job search, our neighbor Estelle asked if she would be interested in a temporary part-time position with her employer, Southwestern Bell. She jumped at the chance. After a short time, she was offered a permanent full-time position in the comptroller's department. Not only did she like what she was doing, she made a lot of friends quickly. She got regular raises as well as other company perks, such as company stock ownership. Because we lived on primarily my salary, she was able to save almost everything she made. This was a time of high interest rates- as much as 16% on some CDs- and she invested our money in those. This served us well later.

A couple of months after I was fully engaged and involved with that exciting project in Houston, Larry White's executive secretary in Fort Worth somehow tracked me down and phoned to ask if I would consider returning. I asked about "Igor," and she said he was no longer in good standing at the firm. I told her I would discuss it with my wife and get back to her later. Gayle and I came to the decision that, while this could be a great opportunity, Igor was still with Larry's firm and the conflict could start again. Besides, we had just gone through the trauma of moving all the way to Houston, had just settled into a new home and were becoming reestablished once again. Returning to Fort Worth would mean another move. In addition, Houston had more opportunities and the economy was booming. I called back the following day and informed the secretary that I considered it an honor to have been asked back but I was in the middle of a major project and could not abandon it at that time.

My new employer engaged the services of a professional architectural model maker who produced a magnificent model of the building. It was about ten feet long. Everybody flocked to the room in which it was displayed and it was depicted in the newspaper and eventually made it into the professional architectural journals. A short time after I finished the schematic design for the bus maintenance facility (every project passes through three phases: Schematic Design, Design Development and Construction Drawing), the project architect resigned. He went on to start his own firm before the next two phases began.

My sketches must have caught the eye of the department head because he told me he had decided to assign the project to me. I thanked him for his confidence in my limited abilities and told him I had never been a project architect in charge of an assignment of that size and my experience up until then was in preparing construction drawings and design. I had no exposure to building codes, client relations, team leadership or developing specs. He said he had every confidence that I would acquire those skills during the course of the project!

This was a major project for a building, with a construction budget of $27 million (in 1980s' dollars). It was an industrial building, a type I had never been exposed to. On top of that, the project was staffed by a group of draftsmen with no experience. Only one had a degree but he was fresh out of school, hadn't taken the registration exam yet or worked anywhere before this project. To add another level of complexity, because the project was partially funded by the federal government, our firm had to select an associate minority firm. The one they chose was located in Austin. This was done in order to conform to a newly mandated federal law enacted to fight discrimination against the few minority firms engaged in architecture. Theoretically, that firm's team was under our supervision. In reality, they were paid by the Austin firm and were, therefore, harder to manage. No wonder not a single project architect, who had been with our firm longer than I, was willing to take it on. They did not want to try to lead an inexperienced team on a project this size under these circumstances, especially since it had been going on for so long and they were not familiar with its history. In addition, they may have assumed the minority firm would be problematic.

There were now six team members from our office, including me, and three from the associated firm, including an undereducated new immigrant from Africa. I chose an Israeli member of our office to act as the job captain. He was older and surer of himself than the rest. I suspect he had been in the Israeli army before he immigrated. I also chose him to let him know that I, an Egyptian whose country was still at war with Israel, held no ill will toward him. However, he did not seem to hold any hostile feelings toward me. He told me he had never been a job captain before and was not sure what it entailed. I explained that he was to make sure everybody had assignments and to tell me if there were problems that needed my attention. I also told him I had every confidence he could do it, the same song and dance the head of the department had told me when I expressed doubt about my abilities. My strategy worked. He managed the team and enabled me to concentrate on developing the drawings. At one point, he told me the minority team was dissatisfied and that I should meet with them to discuss their problems. I told him to ignore them because I was too busy to fool with their unwarranted complaints. Looking back, I know I should have met with them; however, we were approaching a deadline and I did not have the time to waste on meetings to discuss peeves that had no basis. I was lucky because the complaint originated from their leader who just wanted to feel important. He probably went back to his home office, and the owner told him not to rock the boat and cause problems that might jeopardize a lucrative arrangement.

The entire team, including me, learned a lot from working on that project. After finishing the Construction Drawing phase, I convened a meeting and complimented them on their effort and suggested we go out for pizza and beer at a roller skating rink. I paid all expenses without reimbursement from the firm because I was afraid the management might refuse if I should ask. We had a great time and I got lucky because I didn't fall on my butt. In due course, we finished the project on time and under budget. It won an award from the local chapter of the AIA (American Institute of Architects) and was captioned in all the major architectural journals. I thought the firm would be appreciative because of the successful outcome, but I was disappointed when all the credit was given to the electrical engineer who managed the project and interfaced with the management and client's representatives. The firm then assigned me to work under a less experienced architect on an ongoing project. I felt humiliated, underpaid and reached the conclusion there was no future for me in an engineering firm. I had no idea it was standard practice that, as soon as one project was finished, the people who were working on it had to be given something to work on until another project was started and so, were simply assigned to fill whatever openings were available in ongoing projects. Of course, the head of the department could have explained this to me, but he didn't.

I started sending out my upgraded résumé to several major firms in Houston and was granted interviews with a few. My best interview was with Lloyd, Jones and Brewer, one of the more prestigious firms specializing in mainly high-rise buildings. The interview went so well the interviewer, David Brewer, asked me why I wanted so little remuneration. Personally, I thought I was being overambitious in requesting a yearly salary $3000 above what I was making at the engineering firm. After we finished our conversation, he told me he would like Arthur Jones, the partner in charge of design, to meet me before they made a final decision. After I had my second interview with that gentleman, who was not as likable as my first interviewer, I was hired. Thinking back, I believe they hired me because I asked for a lesser amount than they were expecting to pay for an architect with my experience.

The firm was headed by the partners, who employed some rather young senior associates to manage the projects. Despite my experience, I was not given any title because I was new to the firm. I had to report to one of those less experienced people. However, I was not hung up on titles and enjoyed the work.

After my trial period, I was entrusted with the design of a twelve-story parking garage in downtown Houston. Mr. Jones usually did not allow anyone else to do design work, but the firm was busy and he had his hands full with the design of the high-rise office tower for which the parking garage was an adjunct. I did all the design and working drawings as well as allocated time to do the finishing touches. Unexpectedly, I was informed that a sizeable number of staff members, were to be assigned to finish the project. They included associates who outranked me. It was an added burden for me since that group was unfamiliar with the drawings. However, I bit the bullet and allocated tasks to each, and somehow the project was completed without any major snafus.

Mr. Lloyd, the CEO, was an amiable man in his eighties. He was well-to-do when he started his career as a theatrical actor in the Thirties then switched to architecture. He had eccentric tendencies; for example, he bought a new Mercedes-Benz convertible for his young executive secretary as a surprise Christmas present. She was a married woman! The atmosphere in that firm was much more pleasant than the one I left. Each Christmas at a fancy party, David, who was also the president of the company, gave a speech which included a report on the projects he expected to sign a contract on for the coming year as well as the overall financial condition of the firm. He loved making these announcements and being in the spotlight. He did a great presentation and made sure a sizable bonus was distributed based on performance. The party had all the ingredients for boosting morale and encouraging us to do even better in the following year.

During my three years with that firm, I was assigned to several other projects under different project managers. The work was varied and interesting and the yearly office party was festive. I got to go with Gayle and we enjoyed the plentiful fare which included excellent food and drinks. The final party I attended included a prediction from David that tough times were coming soon due to the imminent economic downturn and because the developer who provided the firm with the bulk of its work was taking a "wait and see" position. This did not bode well for me and I updated my résumé in anticipation of the coming layoffs. Oddly enough, a month or two of sporadic layoffs passed before my turn came. It was almost a relief after all the worry and suspense. Shortly afterward, David left to join another firm.

I applied at several firms and landed a job with Calhoun, Tungate, Jackson & Dill, one of the oldest firms in Houston at the time. It was a much smaller firm, less known than the one I left. I had to accept a lesser salary but the office was closer to home so my commute was shorter, which was a boon. I worked at that firm for three years on several projects including a huge church (in Houston, several churches had more than 1000 members at that time) before the firm experienced a scarcity of work and started laying off people. In an effort to retain their most experienced staff, the partners stopped drawing their own salaries in hopes of waiting out the economic downturn and once again finding new projects. However, after we finished all the projects which were in progress, they had to start laying off even those who had been with the firm for many years.

During our time in Houston, we lived through a fierce hurricane. I had seen hurricanes in movies, but experiencing one was something else altogether. Thankfully, we had plenty of warnings and were able to prepare for it. The howling wind, lightning and lashing rain were frightening. After what seemed like an eternity of intense storm, a dead calm occurred. I went out in the backyard and straightened the young Chinese tallow trees we had planted there. The soaked ground and extreme winds had pushed them to a leaning position. After I went back inside, the hurricane resumed in the opposite direction; the lull was only the eye of the storm passing over! We were among the lucky few whose electricity never failed. In fact, our block was the only one in our entire neighborhood that did not lose this vital utility. Many areas of the city were without electricity for weeks due to electric lines felled by tree limbs and other debris. After the hurricane I visited downtown and saw the damage to the high-rise window walls. The destruction was caused by the high wind picking up gravel used as ballast on lower roofs and flinging it into the windows.

Chapter 5
UNFORTUNATE CAREER MOVES

As a hedge against the constant ebb and flow of the economy that seemed to result in my being laid off periodically, Gayle and I attended a real estate seminar which described the way to buy houses and sell them to become rich in no time (Ha Ha). It was an all-day affair that pictured the process as a sure way for untold riches. It sounded so easy, feasible and convincing. The handout described how to do it and provided samples of rental agreements and other forms. We decided to buy a house in our neighborhood and rent it, charging enough to pay most of the mortgage for each month. We were now landlords! We thought we would eventually make a profit from the sale of the house. Because Gayle's work hours at Southwetern Bell were flexible, she carpooled with four other women who liked to begin their day early. That meant she was home by mid-afternoon, allowing her to do all the rental house paperwork, interview potential tenants, check their credit, etc. We did all our own maintenance and repairs on weekends.

This worked well so we decided to buy a second and third houses. We worked hard to accommodate our tenants, so it was frustrating when, at times, we rented to a deadbeat and had to go through the long, costly and complicated process of evicting them. In one instance, we tried everything we could to help the family stay in the house, taking partial payments and even late payments. However, when their checks bounced and when no effort was made to pay the rent at all, we had to bear the cost of going to court to evict them. This was in addition to losing the revenue that would have covered the mortgage payment. We realized the laws were engineered to side with the deadbeats. Of course, the presenters at the seminar never mentioned this aspect of the operation.

Gayle's job

In 1986, when oil prices dropped, Houston went into a tailspin. The entire economy of the city and state plummeted. This, plus the breakup of AT&T into the "Baby Bells," resulted in a huge layoff at Southwestern Bell. It eventually caught up with Gayle when everyone in her unit with less than sixteen years of service with the company was riffed. There were so many people out of work that whenever she got an interview, she was told she was one of the lucky ones just because she had gotten an interview! After a couple of months and numerous disappointments, Gayle went for an interview in a high-rise in Greenway Plaza. She was offered a job in the accounting department of a holding company that controlled oil field equipment companies as well as a high-class gentleman's club– quite a combination! They told her up front she would never have to visit the club but would be doing the payroll for the dancers. At about the time Gayle was settling into her new job, I was laid off. Our foray into real estate was not at a point it would produce income to live on. While we were thankful for Gayle's new job, she had taken a 50% salary cut. Even though we lived frugally we were supplementing our income from savings while hoping the economic situation would improve, but it didn't. I remained unemployed in spite of conducting an active job search in Texas. After about three months, I could no longer stand the idleness, so I went to the library and looked in the want ads in newspapers for cities elsewhere in the country.

Once I took my job search outside the "Oil Belt" I got responses to my inquiries accompanied with plane tickets. I interviewed in

Kalamazoo, MI, Nashville, TN and Winston-Salem, NC. My interview with the firm of Farnsworth & Hopkins (fictional names) in Winston-Salem went very well. Walter Farnsworth was very personable and smooth. He gave me the impression that his firm would pave the way for my advancement and asked if I would be willing to meet with his senior associates to get acquainted. Of course, I agreed. These gentlemen were in their early thirties, brash and self-assured. Again, at 57 years of age, I was being outranked by much younger people with less experience. While I didn't like to be supervised by novices, it was better than staying at home doing nothing. Walter drove a hard bargain when it came to salary negotiations, but I finally agreed on a salary which was somewhat low but acceptable to me under the circumstances. I was not in a good position to bargain. He promised to help me by locating an apartment for us to rent while we concluded our affairs in Houston. This would save us from having to make another trip to look for housing. It was to be a temporary arrangement until we found a house. So I felt comfortable about leaving the choice to him.

I went home and told Gayle the good news but she was crestfallen about having to move yet again and losing her job which she was beginning to feel comfortable with and enjoying. Add to that the fact we would be moving so far away from her family. I pointed out to her that we could not continue to live hand to mouth or use up all our savings while trying to wait out a seemingly interminable recession in Houston and that we had no choice. We had to figure out what to do with the four rental houses plus the house we occupied in a housing market that forced innumerable owners to declare bankruptcy or to vacate their properties and leave the keys under the welcome mat. Thankfully, an acquaintance of Gayle's was a retired fellow who served as a property manager for several owners in order to supplement his pension. We hired him to take care of the maintenance and vacancies as they occurred not only of our rental houses, but for our own home as well, since there was no chance we could sell it in that depressed market. We packed our possessions, hired a mover, stuffed the car and set out to go north. Since it was February, as we got closer to North Carolina we saw snow on the ground and started to wonder just what we had done to ourselves. Living in a place where it snowed was completely foreign to both of us.

Unfortunately, one of our first experiences in North Carolina was a precursor of things to come. On the day we moved into the apartment, we went to a gas station and after I finished refueling, I went to pay using American Express traveler's checks. The owner refused to accept them and belligerently told me he accepted cash only (There were no posted signs to that effect). This was totally unexpected since we had traveled across the country on numerous occasions including our drive from Houston to North Carolina and used them everywhere without a problem. The cash I had was not sufficient to cover the bill, so I asked whether he would make an exception. He answered:

"You will pay me cash or I will take a taar aarn (tire iron) to your windshield."
It was impossible to reason with such an ignorant and primitive personality, so I asked:
"Why don't you call the police?"

My rationale was that I could talk to a policeman and reason with him rather than talk to that oaf. But he told me to call them myself if I wanted to. I had no way to do so and had to leave Gayle standing at the curb outside the station as collateral and drive to the closest bank to get him his precious cash. I doubt he would have behaved that way if he was dealing with a local.

The apartment

After we had settled in the apartment, Walter, who had just divorced his wife of many years, met us accompanied with and his pretty, young fiancé and invited us to a very nice French restaurant. The food was excellent, the host was gracious and the conversation was interesting. Both Gayle and I were very positively impressed. During our talk, we expressed our qualms about the cold and snow; he told us the weather in that area of the country was mild, it seldom snowed and when it did, the white stuff did not stay on the ground for long. The following winter, it snowed heavily and the snow stayed on the ground for two days. It prevented us from going to work. I later jokingly reminded Walter about his statement and he said that this was a freak season. It probably was.

The apartment, which was actually a two-level condo, was in a good location between Greensboro and Winston-Salem in the small town of Kernersville. While it provided us with the storage area we needed as well as allowed us to keep our little dog, it was depressing and not worth the rent. The walls were thin and did not provide the sound isolation we were accustomed to and the finishes were cheap. Our plan was to live there six months to give us time to learn about the area while Gayle looked for a job. Her search was successful in Winston Salem also so, we started looking for a house. In due course, our realtor showed us a ranch-style house in a nice neighborhood. It was on a beautiful open lot that backed up to a small hill with many large mature trees.

Winston-Salem

Like most houses in Winston-Salem at the time, the windows were rather small and the style was dated. It had a cheerful formal living-dining room at the front of the house which we never used and a gloomy den off the kitchen with dark paneling which Gayle hated. The kitchen cabinets were dark and ugly. As soon as we were settled, I started fabricating kitchen cabinet doors and installing them on the weekends. The new birch cabinet fronts gave it a much brighter look. We also changed the dark simulated flagstone flooring to an off-white vinyl which made the room look larger and more cheerful. We completed the remodeling by replacing the old avocado-colored range with a new white one to match the new refrigerator. The changes made a huge difference

This was a time of transition for both of us. North Carolina has a distinctive dialect which made it sometimes difficult to understand their conversations, even for Gayle. One day, we were heading for an address we were not familiar with and stopped to ask a fellow at a store for directions. He said, "Go past the "*taar*" place and it is at the next corner". Since I had never heard of a store that sold tar, I asked him to repeat it a couple of times before we left. We drove on looking for a sign on a store indicating tar was sold there but couldn't find any. However, Gayle noticed a store that sold tires (*taars* in NC lingo) and it dawned on us that it was the store he meant! We still laugh about the "*taar*" store!

The new job
At the office, I started work on a $22 million project for the University of North Carolina. The firm had never been entrusted with a project of that size and complexity. The client mandated a world-famous Canadian architectural firm as a design consultant. I was initially hired as a project architect because I had much more experience with large projects than the senior associates. I was the only one assigned to the project. Normally, a project of that size would require at least four or five interns to produce the drawings. This was either because they didn't know how to handle a sizable project or Walter

wanted to save money as well as test my potential.

Before Halloween that year, an announcement was made stating there would be a costume party at the house of one of the senior associates. Gayle and I improvised our costumes. I went as The Grand Sultan using a yellow towel to fashion an impressive looking turban and a lounging robe over a turtleneck. Gayle went as a Harem Princess using a native dress (*gallabia*) she had bought when we were in Egypt. When we arrived, we found several ingenious characters including Walter in a red cape. He said he had come as a Hot Flash. The host had a store bought costume including a hospital gown open at the back to show a fake bare butt. He was dragging a stand with an IV connected to his arm. His wife accompanied him as an attending nurse. The lady in charge of interior design arrived as a bunch of grapes. She covered her body with green balloons. Everybody had a good time.

The Grand Sultan   The Harem Princess

After I finished the Design Development Phase of the University of North Carolina project, the associate in charge of managing the project told me he, Walter and I would be traveling to Vancouver, Canada to review the work being done by Arthur Erickson & Associates, the Canadian firm the following week. Having lived in Central Texas, I did not own a coat that would provide serious warmth so Gayle and I went shopping and purchased a full length all-weather coat with a zip out lining. At the appointed time, we visited the architect's office and met the two people involved in the design and admired the work. The firm's office was located in a building the architect designed. It was a dramatic space with a large, open studio whose high roof was supported by two huge wooden posts that branched at the top like a tree. We left after it grew dark outside and, while crossing the deserted main street downtown on our way back to the hotel, we were surprised when we saw a large raccoon brazenly crossing the street directly in front of us.

The following day, we had some time left before our flight, so we visited another project designed by the same architect. It was the main courthouse complex, a stunning design with a glass-roofed concourse leading to all the different court rooms. We noticed neat white buckets placed in strategic locations partially filled with brackish water. After trying to figure out what they were for, we saw drops of water plopping in and realized they were placed there to catch water leaking from the roof after a rainstorm. Even great designs can be marred by contractor errors or lax supervision during construction or budget constraints. We never found out what the true cause was. On a vacation trip last year, Gayle and I visited that same building and it was as striking as when I visited it last time and the buckets were gone. I am sure a building of that importance and occupied by lawyers would not have such a problem for long.

After our return to Winston-Salem, I worked hard and finished most of the drawings. As usual, three or four inexperienced people, who were not familiar with the work, were added about two weeks before the deadline to finish the project. This meant more work and worry on my part to make sure all the mistakes they made were corrected before presenting the drawings to the owner for approval. We finished the drawings on time and within the budget. I expected Walter to express his appreciation by living up to his hinted promise of promoting me to the position of senior associate or giving me a sizeable bonus but all he did was let the project manager assign me to a new, larger project for a government building. I started sketching and finished the schematic design not knowing the senior associate in charge of the project was developing a design of his own. In other words, he was in direct competition with me. This is usually never done and it did not bode well. When the time came to make the presentation to the client, he invited me to join him but I decided not to compete with him and upset somebody who is, in essence, my boss. He went and presented both designs. The client took about a week to make their decision, and lo and behold, my scheme was the winner. That was rather awkward for him and for the whole leadership of the firm. To make up for the embarrassment, they started to change my design and came up with a less attractive one to save face. I had already had my fun and didn't want to rock the boat. So I tweaked it a little during the design development phase to make it more palatable.

In the meantime, Walter and his original partner dissolved the partnership probably because of personality or financial conflicts. Walter then promoted the senior associates to full partners. That made the gap between them and me even wider. I became extremely uncomfortable and upset. Walter must have sensed he was not doing the right thing by me. His solution was to include me in the psychological evaluation he and his new partners were undergoing to resolve their differences! He probably hoped the psychiatrist would lay some blame on me so he could convince me I should be happy with the status quo. Unfortunately for him, the written analysis of the numerous psychiatric evaluation forms I had to fill showed my behavior was normal. I had never heard of such turmoil in a firm's leadership and didn't want to be associated with an unstable firm like that one. From that moment, I decided to seek employment somewhere else.

Gayle settled into her job at the American Red Cross and became popular. When she came home, she often told me about how scandalized she was when she heard the things people said about African-Americans. She said she didn't even think people thought that way anymore much less said those things out loud. Winston-Salem was a very bad fit for us. A number of its people at that time were bigoted and intolerant of anybody who looked even slightly darker, as I was, or spoke with even a slight accent. Our neighbors, who were Caucasian Catholic and had moved from Baltimore 15 years earlier, told us that the North Carolinians were still fighting the civil war and considered them Yanks (while Maryland was part of the south and its landed gentry owned slaves, martial law was declared to keep it from seceding). They told us it was only recently people in the neighborhood started to accept them and had begun inviting them to their homes. I thought, if they behaved that way to somebody who looked and spoke no differently from them, I definitely did not stand a chance of fitting in.

Discrimination

To cite an example of bigotry, our clothes dryer stopped working on a Sunday evening and we were stuck with a load of very wet freshly washed clothes. Gayle called the laundromat to ask how late they would remain open so we could take the clothes there to put in the dryer. The woman who answered told her they were open until 7 o'clock. It was about 6:00 p.m. so we put the clothes in a hamper and drove the short distance to the end of the street. I preceded Gayle and carried the basket of wet clothes arriving about 6:30 PM. When I opened the door to the laundromat, the woman who operated it frowned and told me testily "No! No! You can't bring that in now, we're closed". At that moment, Gayle appeared behind me and when the woman saw she was white and we were together, she said, "Oh, come on in Honey, we can still get those done". To her, I was part of an alien invasion or even worse, a light colored NEGRO. Some people are just too set in their erroneous ways to change. I am sure larger cities such as Charlotte and Raleigh were more tolerant to a certain extent since they have major universities with foreign students and other diverse ethnic groups. I am sure that such things must have changed since the late eighties.

Seeking alternatives

By now, changing jobs had become routine for me. I sent my updated resume to a firm in Charleston, SC. Not long afterwards, I received an invitation from that firm with an attached round trip plane ticket to come for an interview. I flew there and was met at the airport by two young senior associates who drove me all over the city touting its beauty and attractions. When we reached the office, they showed me the project I would be assigned to and I met the partner in charge who reviewed my portfolio of projects. The interview went well and they offered me the job with good benefits and a nice salary. After the first euphoria about the prospect of leaving Walter's firm, Gayle and I thought that, in all likelihood, there might be similar discrimination in SC to the one I was experiencing in North Carolina. We did not feel we could put ourselves into that situation again.

Moving to North Carolina proved to me that life is full of surprises. Some are good and some are bad. Winston Salem definitely belonged to the latter category in my case. I know that I strived to do my best and fulfilled my part of the deal. The firm, on the other hand was led by a group of selfish people obsessed with buying the latest BMW cars which they referred to as *"Bimmers"*. In fact, a couple of those associates invited me to accompany them to a BMW dealership during our lunch hour to test drive one of those expensive cars for the sole purpose of impressing me with the fact that they made more money than I did. They were that small minded. While my career was moving along up to that point, this was a definite setback.

Chapter 6
ON TO THE FROZEN NORTH

Hearing that the Boston economy was booming, we decided we needed to be in a more metropolitan area offering more employment opportunities. I started sending resumes to several firms there and received an invitation to come for an interview from a well-known firm whose work I had seen in one of the architectural journals. Gayle and I flew there on a weekend and stayed at a downtown hotel. I interviewed with the black founding partner as well as two other firms while Gayle scanned the Boston Globe to find out what the real estate market was like. My interview went very well and he offered me a job with an acceptable salary and agreed to pay half the cost of our move.

We had the rest of the day free so, we decided to explore the city and enjoy the sights. Boston is a beautiful city with wonderful scenery including high-rises, world class museums and an interesting harbor area. On the spur of the moment, we bought two tickets on a Hop-on Hop-off bus tour. The driver who was also the tour guide was a really funny guy who told us stories about the neighborhoods we passed through and included funny remarks about people who happened to be inattentive and crossed the path of the bus. We enjoyed his travelogue and used that bus all day visiting some of the attractions of the city including the world-famous Faneuil Hall and Quincy Market which is a delightful shopping mall full of interesting eateries, street performers and historical sites. It is visited every year by millions of tourists. We also decided to take a harbor cruise.

When we arrived at the pier, what was a warm day suddenly turned very cold with a shift in the wind so we purchased sweatshirts at an inflated price in order to survive. Boy, did they feel great as we slipped them on... almost worth the price! We enjoyed these activities and were thoroughly impressed by the city.

We returned to Winston-Salem realizing that moving to Boston was the right course of action to take. Based on that decision, we started planning our move. Gayle was sad about leaving her job but said she felt we had made a mistake in moving to a small town. We put our house up for sale and started packing. We also planned another trip to Boston to look for a place to live. At the same time we contacted a real estate agent who arranged for us to see several apartments and homes so that when we arrived in Boston for our home search, we could hit the ground running. We arrived mid-day on a Friday and had until Monday evening to find a new place to live. A rental car gave us the flexibility to see a wide area.

The agent showed us several apartments in Brookline which were in an awful state of disrepair. Add to this the fact there was only on-street parking requiring us to to move the cars somewhere else each time the snow plows came. We could not imagine how anybody would have the audacity to offer them for rent at such inflated rates. However, our thought was, since we were making such a huge change in our lives, it might be interesting to live within the city rather than the suburbs. We soon concluded that our money allocation for rent was insufficient at the monthly rates they were asking, in those close-in neighborhoods. In between appointments we visited an ice-cream shop for a treat and were feeling rather down about what we had seen so far.

We spread a map of the area on our table and started talking to a man there who asked if he could help when he saw us poring over it. We explained our situation and he told us about nice small towns adjoining Boston proper that might be more budget-friendly, mentioning Canton, Norwood, Dedham and Easton. That evening, Gayle found an ad in the paper about a condo complex within our budget in Canton which is about 30 miles south of Boston. We drove south the next day to the address indicated and found it was a brand new development and realized that it was exactly what we needed.

The newly built condo we visited had two bedrooms, 2 1/2 baths and a lot of storage space in the basement, a one-car garage which was lacking in all the others we had seen and the back opened onto a small private area that flowed into a wooded expanse. It also had pretty landscaping and was only two blocks from a commuter rail station. However, we were not quite ready to give up our idea of living closer to Boston and saw several other places. Monday morning came and we had a "Eureka moment", looked at one another and said, "It's Canton!" We drove back to the development and spoke to the on-site representative explaining that we wanted to sign a lease so we could give the moving company an address for delivery. The condo manager said they would have to check our credit before they accepted us as tenants. Gayle, being wise in the ways of real estate dealings, wrote a check for the deposit and the first month's rent on the spot saying we had little time for all that since we had a plane to catch.

Back in Winston-Salem, our answering machine had a message from the firm I had interviewed with in Charleston asking me to call back. I talked to one of my interviewers and told him I was leaning toward accepting an offer from the Boston firm. He told me he would call me back after he conferred with the partner. Half an hour later, he called back and made me a higher offer than the Boston firm. Based on that figure, I called the Boston office and told the vice-president about the offer from S.C. He reluctantly agreed to match it. I communicated that fact to the office in SC and they made me an even higher offer! It was so great to feel I am worth all that. When they made a follow-up call to find out when I could start work. I told him I had accepted the offer from the other firm because I felt Boston would provide more opportunities for both Gayle and me. He tried to get me to change my mind by saying they were ready to raise their offer but I told him it was not a question of money. Later that morning, the Canton condo management called and informed us everything was in order and the apartment was ours. That was the last loose end and we thanked God for smoothing out all the obstacles.

I gave my two weeks notice which was not graciously accepted. They acted as if I was disloyal for leaving them on the lurch which was untrue since I had completed the project. I suppose they thought I was going to see it through the construction phase. At that point, I could not have cared less about what happened to the project or the firm. They acted as if I was ungrateful and scrambled to find a replacement for me. I bit the bullet for the remainder of the two weeks and was glad to be rid of that place. It took me eleven months of correspondence and a threatening letter before I got them to pay what was due to me from my 401k. That was their gratitude for the tremendous effort I did to finish a project not only on time but also within budget. That was outside their level of experience.

Gayle arranged for the move and contacted the real estate agent who found the Winston-Salem house for us originally and arranged for the sale. After the movers had loaded all our belongings, we started our drive to Boston stopping in

Baltimore along the way to see the beautiful, rejuvenated harbor there and visit the aquarium. Arriving ahead of the movers, we got the condo keys and slept fitfully on an air mattress on the floor that first night in order to be there when the movers came. All the furniture was set up and most of the boxes were put into the basement. I went to the office soon after and we continued to unpack a little at a time.

Once we were settled in, Gayle started her job search. She applied at several companies and found a number of somewhat interesting positions. She did not want a long commute so kept her search within the immediate area. On several occasions, the director at the Red Cross in North Carolina called to urge her to apply at the Red Cross in Boston. She hesitated to do so because, being a non-profit organization, she was paid so little in NC. She didn't want to struggle for each small raise as she did there where her director had to go to bat for her to get a 5 cent an hour increase. While she loved knowing she was doing something good for others, she also realized she needed to build up her savings and social security for later. To tie that loose end and respond to her insistent caller, she set an appointed to interview at the Red Cross office in Dedham, a small town close by.

She discovered the headquarters of the New England American Red Cross Blood Services was only 7 miles from our condo. She soon found the pay scale at that Red Cross unit was much different from what she received in NC. She applied for one of several job openings and was invited for an interview with the director of the education group which, not surprisingly, went very well. They made her an offer which included a reasonable salary with good benefits as well as counted her employment time at her former ARC job toward her overall service time. Adding those one and a half years up front gave her more vacation and sick time quicker. Later, that added period made her eligible for retirement after a shorter interval than if her time in NC was wasted. This was yet another example of God's benevolence.

The Boston architectural firm I joined was not organized like any other office I had worked for. In fact, calling it organized is an exaggeration. I discovered the office was actually run by the junior partner who was absent during my interview. He was not pleased about the fact he was not consulted even though I was hired by the founder of the firm. I was assigned trivial tasks and placed under the supervision of someone who was not even a registered architect. I bit the bullet and reasoned I was not in a position to rock the boat so soon after being hired. Eventually something interesting would come my way. I figured that this, being a minority firm, was not in a position to lay me off quickly because they would not be able to attract many people with my experience and qualifications. There was always a chance an opening might occur in a more prestigious firm once I became familiar with their building code and how things were done in Boston.

My first book
To occupy myself during lax times, I started writing a technical book based on my long experience. It was interesting research work and I prepared all the illustrations and the accompanying text until I was satisfied with the result. To test whether publishers would be interested, I wrote a table of contents and an explanation of why it would be of interest to architects and sent it to some of the major publishers of architectural books. I was extremely excited when I received the responses and found two major publishers were interested enough to send me forms to fill out to elaborate on several issues pertaining to content, qualifications, target audience, competing books, etc. I sent the

completed forms back and received phone calls from the editors to discuss remuneration and the desired time for completion.

I chose Van Nostrand Reinhold and signed a contract because I had seen their impressive list of published books. I thought I had found the road to my salvation from the treadmill of working for firms that did not appreciate me such as the one I was currently working for. I set to work giving up evenings, weekends, holidays and vacations to meet the deadlines. Gayle did more than her share. She had to decipher my tiny handwriting, redo the typing whenever I amended the text. She worked as hard as I did, all this, in addition to working full-time and taking care of most of the household chores. She is a remarkable woman and I am very lucky to have married her. Little did I know that publishing a technical book, unlike novels, is designed to enrich the publisher and not the author who toils long hours to perfect the content. The contract is designed to offer 12% or less of the net sale price (the money the publisher gets after discounting the price to bookstores and marketing, etc.). When books are sold through book clubs, foreign sales and mail order, the author gets 5%.

Publishers, as I learned later on, execute the bulk of the sales through the latter category. In essence, the author does the bulk of the difficult work based on his or her unique knowledge and the publisher gets 95% of the revenue for emending the language, producing the book and advertising. It is a totally unfair operation, so much for finding an alternative type of work. This tremendous effort was not a total loss, however. It made the firm principals sit up and take notice of my potential value as a marketing tool for their services. Whenever they sent in their qualifications to compete for a project, they sent in my resume and included the fact that I wrote that book. They even gave me a puny raise to keep me on the staff. Once they secured the job, they almost never assigned it to me! The government entity that entrusted the project to the firm never checked whether I was involved in it or not.

Because of the high cost of housing in the Boston area, we never thought we would be able to afford a home there. When we looked at prices in the paper, it took our breath away. So we renewed out lease and since it did not increase, we were happy. The following year, however, when the time to renew arrived, we got a letter saying the developer was working to sell all the units to raise capital and our lease would not be renewed. The letter urged us to bid on the condo we were occupying and it listed the asking prices for the various units. It was a dilemma! The prices in the letter were out of our budget range as we were still in sticker shock at the cost of real estate in the area. However, we had to have a place to live so we started exploring other developments by other builders. We liked his more modern designs and well-done interiors of the condo we lived in.

One Sunday afternoon, we were looking at an apartment in our development which was not far from where we were living. When we finished touring the model, we asked the receptionist if that builder had any other developments in the area. She said, "I am not sure so why don't you ask him" just as a man walked through the door. We introduced ourselves and told him where we lived and why we were touring the apartment complex. He asked if we liked where we were living and we said yes but that we could not afford to buy it. He smiled and said, "Make me an offer. I think you might be surprised." We went home and started formulating our strategy! We made an offer and it was countered. We countered and held our breath. The acceptance came with a caveat – the price could not be lowered further to keep the value of the other units intact but the builder would pay all our closing costs! Once again God's hand was there for us and we had a permanent home.

After being at the firm for six years, it experienced a cash-flow crisis during an economic downturn. The junior partner who had always had an antipathy toward me trumped up an accusation that I was undermining the authority of a favorite project architect that he had recently hired and I was laid off. I had to scramble to think of what I would do next. I applied to a firm and was told I was overqualified. A standard reply for older applicants (I was 64 years old at that time) who would expect a higher salary than the firm was prepared to offer. I knew that going that route would entail a lot of rejections, frustrations and wasted time and effort so I decided to try to establish a consulting business.

To research that possibility, I went to a bookstore and found a book entitled, "Inside the Technical Consulting Business" written by Harvey Kaye, an engineer. It gave me pointers on what steps to take to make it happen. Following the recommendations of that book, I cut out some of the details from the last project I had checked as a project architect and marked them with red lines highlighting the errors and coordination conflicts. I included these marked details in a brochure I designed. Gayle used her computer savvy to scan the details and format the text to produce the brochure which we then copied. Gayle set up a database with names and addresses and printed covering letters and envelopes. We mailed 50 copies of the brochures describing the advantages my checking would confer on a firm along with my resume. I also described other services such as developing details and checking specifications that would be advantageous to an architectural firm.

There were no responses since this type of service had only been offered before by a very expensive firm specializing in project forensics to pinpoint non-coordination and remedial work on buildings that had problems. Only rich owners, contractors and government entities contracted with that firm. Architects are very conservative in their decision-making process and hate to take risks. They also considered the services I outlined as something that should be done in-house by the project architect. In practice, this in-house checking almost never happens because no time is allocated specifically for that activity and very few firms have people with the experience to do a good job of checking. However, the idea of outsourcing work in some areas was gaining acceptance in other cities, so I decided to continue. After a couple of weeks of following each mailing with a call to see if direct contact would bring results, I decided to follow a new strategy.

I called a major firm and offered to present a free technical seminar at their office during the lunch hour and referred to the brochure I sent. Two or three offices took the bait and even though standing up in front of a group of people who were more interested in eating and taking a nap was not the easiest undertaking, I did a pretty good job of presenting my educational information. I met afterwards with one of the principals who agreed to let me do the quality check on one of his projects at a ridiculously low fee. However, that client gave me several subsequent assignments and it started the ball rolling. During intervals between projects, I continued to market my services and included a list of projects I was in charge of. More firms became interested and assigned projects to me. It was hard work requiring extreme focus but I loved being independent and on my own. Gayle's job provided us with health insurance and a reliable supplemental income that sustained us during gaps between assignments. Gayle also came up with a letterhead using a logo I designed for the business. She then used the logo on all the business forms she prepared such as contract agreements, fax cover letters, invoices and late payment letters.

A new job
During one of my marketing calls, I contacted an acquaintance I met at a technical seminar given by an expert on exterior wall design. That acquaintance was a senior associate in one of the best known firms in Boston. I asked if he would use his influence to invite me to make my presentation. He called back and told me when to come. On the appointed day, I took a portfolio of the projects I had been entrusted with and a copy of the technical book I wrote. I made my presentation and the interview with a partner afterwards went well. He asked me what I would charge to check a project he was leading and we agreed on a sum. However, they wanted me to work at their office which meant I was once again commuting into Boston by train. My work was appreciated and the first assignment was followed by a stream of major projects given to me for checking. Gayle took care of preparing the contracts, all the invoicing and tax paperwork. In essence, Gayle acted as the office manager for the business and from time to time even called offices to request payment for services when they were late.

After two or three months performing checks for that firm, the vice president in charge of hiring offered me a permanent job doing what I had been doing as a consultant. This was done at the prompting of the associate whom I first contacted. His role in the firm was to manage quality control and educate the staff. My impression was that the VP was not enthusiastic about making the offer. Some people just develop an antipathy toward me without being based on anything I had done. I call that tendency "The Winston-Salem Effect". However, the offer provided me with a sure salary instead of having to constantly market my checking service as a consultant, so I accepted.

After working for a year and a half, the economy hit a rough spot and I was told to work on a project presided over by a young project architect for whom I had checked a project or two and had found many, many errors. This, of course, was an unacceptable situation because that assignment could be used as a precedent to make me work on other projects under junior architects. In essence, it amounted to a big demotion. Consequently, I told the senior associate I worked with that I would rather take an unpaid leave until the firm started to get busy again. He agreed and I returned to work at home as a consultant to other firms. It was a lean time but I was able to land a few projects.

A new book
Inevitably, there were periods of idleness so I decided to write another technical book. This time it would be a book related to the technical aspects of building construction. After I finished a sizable part of the book, I decided to test whether publishers would be interested. I sent the outline to several major publishers and received several answers expressing interest and inviting me to submit a formal proposal based on a standard format to be evaluated by a senior editor. Again, I received several letters of interest, I chose McGraw-Hill, a firm known for their technical publications. I negotiated the terms the best I could after having a publishing attorney look at the agreement but publishers are a tough breed. I was able to bump the compensation marginally and started working enthusiastically on the book writing and revising it continuously. The advance I received helped with our expenses. Halfway through writing the book, I received a letter from the firm that granted me the "unpaid vacation" informing me my employment had been terminated "by mutual consent"! I had given no such consent. I thought about suing them for laying me off due to my advanced age but knew it would be a frustrating,

long drawn out and expensive proposition with an uncertain outcome, so, I decided to continue my work as a consultant.

Income from my consulting services and Gayle's salary at the Red Cross kept us going. I sent sections of the book as soon as I finished them to the editor for review and amendments. Gayle did all the typing and re-typing from my scribbled handwriting. Finally I finished the book which was entitled *Time-Saver Details For Exterior Wall Design* after working furiously every minute in between consulting projects and it was published. I then started receiving accounting reports every six months showing how many books were sold in the US, through book clubs and to foreign countries. The first five accounting reports of sales were credited to the publisher to pay back the $5000.00 advance payment they sent after I signed the contract . Finally, I started receiving my percentages. While the money came in handy, the compensation amounted to about one tenth of what my hourly rate was when I worked in a firm and even less when compared to my consultant fees. On the plus side, mentioning the book to prospective users of my consulting business was a powerful tool which made convincing them to use my services easier. In this sense, the book was not a total business calamity.

Each year, I increased my hourly rate by $5 and found this did not affect the volume of work. I loved the independence that resulted from being on my own including the freedom to determine the time I took off for a vacation to coincide with Gayle's. An added bonus was the short and sweet commute from the bedroom to the room I designated as an office in our condo. No rushing to catch a train or trudging in the snow, slush and ice to reach the office. The people I interacted with were respectful and appreciative and the rewards contrasted very favorably with what I used to make. I wished I had shifted to consulting a long time before. During my lunch breaks, I took daily walks that lasted half an hour. I used those occasions to have a conversation with God. It was uplifting and gave me an opportunity to express my gratitude for all the blessings He had bestowed on me and seek His guidance when I was confronted with a challenge. This habit has taken root and I still practice it before lunch with Gayle.

Seminars

To increase my exposure and make it easier to attract new client firms, I started volunteering to give seminars at the yearly Build Boston symposium. At first, I was very nervous about facing a crowd of strangers staring at me. But I armed myself with technical slides I developed to draw those eyes away from me and make my presentation easier to understand, it worked beautifully. The executive director of the symposium informed me during one of our chance encounters that my seminars drew the largest number of attendees! A couple of them drew more than 200 architects. I was delighted and prepared seminars dealing with other technical subjects that I knew were much needed. I presented those seminars about three more times.

Boston natives

One of the things we noticed when we moved to the Boston area was that the people were not as friendly as Texans. Often after being confronted by an antagonistic person, I would simply ask them if I had done something to upset them. Their answer was always a baffled and gruff, "No." After thinking about it, I reached the conclusion that its population was naturally combative. They were divided among several disparate groups residing in well-defined neighborhoods. The Irish lived in a south side enclave called Southie, the Italians lived in their North End, Jews and Blacks had their own enclaves and all the know you, however, they became friendlier. We made many wonderful friends through work and church. In fact, our church became our family away from home in Texas. We participated in many activities there and even introduced an annual putt-putt golf competition complete with prizes.

Chapter 7
OUR TRAVELS

Each summer during our vacation, we took major trips. In addition, we took several local trips including harbor tours, a dinner train trip on Cape Cod and side trips to New Hampshire, Maine and Vermont. Every fall, the trees in the entire area became clad in amazing colors that delighted our souls. Our first foray abroad was in Canada where we visited Quebec, Montreal and Toronto. After boarding the subway to several points of interest in Toronto, we took the elevator in the famed tower and I went out on the balcony at the top. Gayle followed me and was immediately swept by the strong wind and landed on the floor where she could not get up and before I could do anything, a couple of visitors raised her up. It was a scary situation. Later we visited Quebec and Montreal as part of a bus tour. The two cities were totally different — one metropolitan and the other like a city in Europe. I remember our having lunch at a charming sidewalk restaurant as we watched people passing by.

We also took a trip to Niagara Falls and saw their awesome majesty from both the American and Canadian sides. We visited my niece in upstate New York and toured the campus at Cornell University where her husband taught. We also booked a tour to see Nova Scotia in May... BIG MISTAKE! The weather was chilly and most restaurants were closed because it was before the tourist season. The motels included in that tour were rather distant and we had to reach them in a very narrow slot of time that didn't allow us to tarry much to see the sights. We liked the friendly people and felt like we were in a time warp in one particular small town. It reminded Gayle of the US in the late fifties. Even the music we heard was from that era. We liked that aspect of it and we also liked the Alexander Graham Bell Museum which was impressive. Maybe one day we will revisit that part of Canada during warmer weather.

Other trips included two cruises to Bermuda which we enjoyed thoroughly. The first was a cruise which happened by sheer luck. We had planned a bus trip to Quebec and arranged for our vacations to occur in that time slot. At the eleventh hour, we were informed that the organizer had canceled it. To correct the situation, I went to a travel agent during my lunch hour to find out what she could do for us. The agent said, "Have I got an alternative for you" and gave me a brochure for a dream cruise to Bermuda costing slightly less than the bus trip. We had never been on a cruise before and I was excited at the prospect and phoned Gayle from the agency about it. She readily agreed to the deal and excitedly said, "Take it, take it". We went and had one of the best vacations we ever had up to that moment because it was a mode of travel we hadn't experienced and Bermuda was so different and interesting.

World travelers
We now had the wherewithal to see the world and since flights from Boston to Europe and Egypt are closer than those from cities in Texas, we decided to spend our vacations traveling to those destinations. Our first trip was a guided bus tour of Europe where we visited seven countries in fourteen days. The tour director was a strict disciplinarian who informed us on the first day the bus would leave every morning at 7 o'clock sharp and stragglers would have to arrange for their own transportation to catch it at the following stop in another country. That trip was not a vacation, it felt more like

punishment, however, we were exposed to more countries than we could have visited over a long period of time. To our chagrin, we were unable to visit Florence (*Firenze* in Italian) because unusually heavy rains had caused flooding that year. I wanted to visit the famous Duomo church and the amazing Ponte Vecchio bridge which integrated picturesque shops in its structure.

Among our travel group, were some Australians. They were cheerful and very helpful. Whenever I had trouble pushing Gayle up a hill, one of them would pitch in to help propel the wheelchair. When we arrived at the catacombs, Gayle told me to go ahead because of the many steps leading down to them. One of the Australians heard her and said, "You didn't come all this way to sit and wait for the group to return. You will go even if it means we carry you back up the stairs. It doesn't make sense to come all the way to Rome and miss going there." With that reassurance, down we went. Gayle walked the narrow paths and was happy she was able to see the Christian wall paintings that were centuries old. Those Australians were real gentlemen. We have great respect for them; they are a remarkable people, true "mates".

On a following trip, we flew to Rome and acted as our own travel agent enjoying the unstructured itinerary. We visited the Forum, the Roman Baths of Caracalla, and other points of interest, ate their delightful food and enjoyed their delicious *gelatti* (ice cream). We took a bus tour and used the subway for longer distances that were too far to walk. I had a phrase book that I used effectively to reach our destinations. Apparently, my pronunciation was good enough to make the people I talked to assume that I was familiar with the language. They gave detailed directions in fast Italian. I understood enough to allow me to head to the first street corner described and collar another unsuspecting native to give me directions and so on until we reached our destination. We found a small deli across the street from our hotel. It served delicious sandwiches on fresh bread. Unfortunately, it did not have a place to sit, so we ate them sitting on a store window sill. Passers by looked oddly at us and must have thought, "look at those poor, crazy tourists". We didn't care, it was fun.

From Rome we took a train and stayed for a week at a two-story farm house in Tuscany (*Toscana* in Italian). My niece Nadia, who was born in Germany, had an Italian boyfriend, Nino, in his late thirties who worked on his father's farm in the area. She arranged for the rent and drove us in her small *Fiat* to places of interest in the region including Pisa, Sienna, Montalcino, Luca and several small and picturesque towns whose names I have forgotten. Nevertheless, that trip was most enjoyable. During our ride, my niece played some Italian songs on the car CD player. She translated them as they were sung, one of those was about Texas cowboys and how they loved to cook their delicious coyotes! It was very funny and we enjoyed the Italian humor. My brother and his wife, who were living at the time in Alsace in France, drove down to stay with their daughter so it was a real family reunion. In the evening we would all sit around the table with different languages flying back and forth – English, Italian, German with an Arabic word thrown in from time to time. My niece did a wonderful job of translating and she had to take a "brain break" from time to time to rest. I was impressed by her quick ability to switch from one language to another.

After our trip to Tuscany, Gayle and I took the train back to Rome and flew to Cairo. This was not long after a terrorist attack on a German bus had resulted in a number of deaths so we looked for alternatives to large group tours such as Grand

Circle Tours or Trafalgar Tours. As part of the trip planning in

Dinner in Tuscany
From left: Ingborg, Naguib, Nino, Nadia and me

Massachusetts, Gayle had contacted an Egyptian travel agency she found on the web to take us to the places they specialized in. We also did not want my family to have to make the long trip to the airport to meet us very late at night when we arrived. The company operated a number of minivans that could carry two couples in addition to the driver. We reasoned that riding in a minivan would be less likely to be a target for the fanatics. However, in my experience, time is viewed a bit differently in the Middle East than in the Western World so I was pleasantly surprised when we saw the travel agent waiting in the customs area with a sign bearing my name. He helped us with our luggage and whisked us quickly into Cairo and our hotel.

Because tourism had been devastated by the terrorist attacks, we were able to stay at the luxurious 5-star "Le Meridien" hotel located at the prow of an island in the Nile at a very reasonable rate because we did not want to impose on my family. The first thing I noticed when we entered our room on the third floor was a service call button next to the door with a caption reading "Bush Button". I thought about it for a minute then I remembered that most Egyptians pronounce the letter "P" as "B"! It should have read, "Push" instead of "Bush". The room had a balcony that we knew we would enjoy. However, it was very noisy because there was a wedding celebration somewhere close which went on past midnight. We called the desk and had them transfer us to a similar room on the eighth floor.

When we opened the door and stepped on the balcony the following morning, the air was so polluted and the visibility was very limited because of the smog. The smell of smoke spoiled the whole impression. When I lived there, the air was pure and visibility was unlimited. Nowadays, the congested roads, the burning of trash and other factors caused that awful condition. So each morning, when we got up, the first thing we did was to go out on the balcony and count the number of bridges across the Nile we could see which gave us a quick indication of how bad the smog would be that day. On other days and in the evening we would gather with all my family. Many nieces and nephews came to greet us. I could not believe how they had grown into young adults with children of their own. I remembered them as young children whom I told stories to. It was a happy gathering. The next day, we visited the Pyramids. Gayle was awed by their size which no photo can capture. They were on a scale similar to that of the Grand Canyon.

One day, two of my brothers and their wives treated us to lunch at their social club. Gayle loved these outings because she got to try all the different foods that were offered with guidance as to the best to choose. She loved the grilled pigeon, the *kabab*

Gayle and Fred at the pyramids

(grilled lamb meat on a skewer), *kofta* (a delicious ground beef dish), a variety of dates, *konafa* (sweet nut and honey dessert wrapped in baked dough similar to shredded wheat) and numerous other dishes of the region. She wanted to try everything! One afternoon Gayle and I dined on the terrace overlooking the Nile at our hotel. The hotel provided a local touch by constructing an adobe oven, at a lower terrace, where a peasant woman sat baking pita bread. It was a tourist attraction. When we ordered our meal, Gayle asked the waiter to substitute the western bread with hot loaves from that woman. He was astonished and asked her several times if she was sure because nobody had made that request before but he complied and we enjoyed it very much because it was something we could never find fresh and hot in the States.

We Also visited the famous Khan-el-Khalili bazaar, a must-see attraction for tourists. Gayle bought a native dress, made-to-order while we waited. She wears it on rare occasions to surprise people. We also saw the Citadel (a fortified mosque built by Saladin between 1176 and 1183) located on a hill visible from many parts of the city. We were required to cover our shoes with canvas booties at the entrance as a sign of respect. The caretaker sheik told us that the domed assembly room had remarkable acoustics that allow the worshipers to hear clearly from any location within that space. Gayle asked me to request a demonstration, so he raised his voice and intoned the *Shehada: "Allahu Akbar"* and he was right, the acoustics were

Peasant woman baking pita bread at the Hotel

impressive. Gayle was thrilled like any tourist would be.

We also visited several interesting destinations including the oldest Coptic (Christian) Church, the Egyptian Museum and the Nile Hilton hotel next door where, before I immigrated, I used to go for coffee in its colorful and cheerful cafeteria. I noticed the approach to the hotel had deteriorated beyond recognition. It used to be a breathtaking modern building designed by Welton Beckett & Associates, a well known American architectural firm. When it opened in the late fifties it had manicured lawns with palm trees. That was the first time instant landscaping, executed in about a week, was introduced to Egypt. It was like a miracle at the time and everybody was wowed by it. The hotel also had great colorful graphics depicting abstract illustrations of Ancient Egyptian themes; it was a destination for tourists and the upper crust of Egyptian society. When we saw it, the lawn area was replaced by a seedy mall of kitschy shops which blocked the view to the entrance. It was such a shame that commercialism had ruined such a distinctive building.

London
Our travels also included a trip to London where we visited the British Museum with its impressive displays including a large section about Egypt. We took a double-decker bus tour of the city. At embassy row, we passed by the Canadian embassy and noticed a Texas flag on an official, eagle-topped flagpole in front of the entry to the back of the building. It had an official-looking sign that read, "EMBASSY OF TEXAS". We looked at each other and said, "Did Texas secede from the union after we left?" When we left the bus, we traced our way back to the area by feel and were lucky to find the building and confirmed the sign was correct. We then noticed the sign had a subtitle in small print that read, "Cantina". It was a Mexican food restaurant! We also visited Harrods department store which amazed us with the diversity and scope of its displays. Calling it a department store is an understatement. It is a department store/butcher shop/ jewelry store/museum and pastry shop. At that time, the British food did not live up to the greatness of the city attractions. The only place we liked was a pub where we had fish and chips washed down with cold ale. It was a distinctively British establishment with a cozy atmosphere and a sign next to the entrance that told of its strange history which included a murder and other interesting details.

On to Paris

The following week we took the EuroRail to Paris and visited the Louvre and Versailles as well as other points of interest using the Metro subway. After a 5 day stay there, we boarded a train and went to Odratzheim in Alsace to visit my brother Naguib and his wife-Ingborg at their beautiful two-story home. They took us to see all their favorite places as well as places they knew we would enjoy. In Freiberg, across the border in Germany, we left their car at a parking lot on the outskirts as required and took the electric train into the city which was all pedestrian. We visited many interesting places there including the beautiful cathedral in the center of the city. When our visit with them was over, we boarded the train again back to Paris and flew home.

Our move to Boston was a very good move for both of us. We lived in Canton for 14 years during which time we saw foreign lands, sampled exotic food and enjoyed the amazing colors during spring and autumn. Of course we had to endure the snow, sleet and ice but I am not going to dwell on that aspect. I advanced professionally and Gayle enjoyed her work and developed several enduring friendships. The Lutheran church we attended was a small one where we enjoyed the sermons of the young pastor and developed many friendships. I felt that God had guided us there after the alienation and frustrations we had experienced in Winston-Salem.

Chapter 8
I RETIRE

After working for five years in my home-office, I decided the time had come for me to retire and move away from the cold of Massachusetts back to Texas. I discussed the thought with Gayle but she told me she liked working for the American Red Cross and did not like the idea of retiring. I was surprised because she had to drive to work in winter and spend about half an hour at the end of the day scraping the ice and snow from the car before she drove home. But she made a strong case for continuing since she had to work for two more years before she became eligible for early retirement. Quitting at that time would have meant she would lose her pension, so I decided to postpone my retirement until she became eligible.

One day I was leafing through the AARP (American Association of Retired People) magazine and found an ad about an active adult retirement community in Texas where prospective home purchasers were invited to stay in one of their fully furnished model homes for $50 a night. I said to Gayle, "Since we are going to visit your parents this fall in Cuero, why don't we fly into Austin, drive to that community and stay for a few nights as part of our vacation trip?" She agreed but expressed hesitancy about staying longer than a couple of nights since we didn't know if we were walking into an uncomfortable situation. We set the date for our vacation and made the reservation.

After the visit with Gayle's parents, we drove north to Austin. It turned out to be a delightful, nicely landscaped development of a few thousand homes. We were impressed from the moment we entered the community. We checked into our assigned vacation home and found it to be fully equipped, clean and well-laid out. It was tastefully furnished and included everything from dishes to a golf-cart in the garage for in-community transportation. Gayle took it for a spin and felt like she was in an amusement park. She had a smile of shear ecstasy whenever she got on that machine. I tried it and it was fun, but I let her drive it throughout our stay because I could not imagine depriving her of that pleasure. I am still a passenger to this day.

The first morning after we arrived, we woke up around six o'clock. Gayle brewed some coffee and we sat on the terrace to watch the peaceful scenery. With my peripheral vision, I perceived a movement at a distance and, lo and behold, we saw a herd of deer walking through the morning mists. It was a dreamy moment. That scene was repeated in the evening when the deer returned across the golf course in the opposite direction. This added to our appreciation of the place. We talked to several people living there and they were all lavish in their praise of their life style. During our exploration of the community in the golf cart, we drove into a picnic area and came upon three deer grazing next to the street. We were about three or four feet from them. They raised their heads, looked at us for a couple of minutes and when we didn't move, they resumed their grazing. We felt like we were in a Disney movie.

When we went to the sales office, we discovered we could actually visit each of the fully furnished model homes on site and we received a package which contained plans for the homes being built at that time and their prices. Their brochure listed all the amenities in the community. Those included clubs for hobbies such as pottery, arts, woodworking, stained glass and several other interesting activities. It had two golf courses something we were not interested in but which kept the development open and well tended as well as several tennis courts and a well equipped fitness center. It had a bank branch, a small grocery store, two restaurants and a medical clinic that could be reached by golf cart. We took the offered minibus tour of the surrounding area as well. The guide showed us the historic town nearby in addition to the retirement community itself.

On the plane back to Massachusetts, we kept saying, "There must be a catch somewhere. This is too good to be true." Gayle jokingly said, "They must have added something to the water to keep people so unanimously content". We decided to go back the next time we visited Gayle's parents to make sure that our first impressions were correct. We excitedly called and reserved a house for five days and four nights six months later. As the months passed we talked more and more about retirement. We pored over each of the house plans and chose one we thought would work for us, both for living and financial feasibility. Gayle looked into her retirement options at work as much as she could, while staying under the radar of the department director because she was concerned if her intent of taking early retirement became general knowledge, she would be side-lined and no longer given additional opportunities. After all, she still had a two years to go before being eligible for early retirement which included health insurance coverage.

Finally, we went back because we were eager to gather as much information as possible, so we stopped everybody we encountered including a lady walking her dog. Gayle asked about her evaluation of the place and she said that it couldn't be better. During their conversation, Gayle mentioned the fact that her handicap was due to childhood polio. The lady said her husband had had polio also and was suffering from post-polio syndrome and she invited us to her house to have coffee! We met her husband and they had a conversation about remedies and problems resulting from the progress of the disease. We stopped a guy riding a bicycle and he also expressed great satisfaction. That settled it! We attended the sales reception given for those who were staying at the vacation homes. Afterwards, we talked to Betty, one of their sales representatives who had a distinctive Texas accent. She led us to a large scale model of the community and showed us the locations of the neighborhoods under construction and where houses conforming to the model we chose would be built.

We explained how important it was for the lot to be level so the house wouldn't have any steps. We were both tired of going up and down the stairs in our three-level condo. This was also driven by Gayle's earlier diagnosis of post-polio syndrome, a return of weakness in the muscles initially affected by the virus after they had partially recovered. Betty seemed to understand our needs and so drove us to inspect lots she deemed to be flat enough that they might not require any steps into the house at the entry or from the garage. I also wanted a lot that had the right orientation to minimize exposure to the intense western sun. We had lived in Austin when we first got married and we knew how hot it could get. I began the conversation which went something like this:

"We are interested in buying one of the houses, the "Long" model."
"You have made an excellent choice. Do you have any questions about it?"
I suspect she said that to all prospective buyers.
I replied, "We think it satisfies most of our needs, can we make modifications to it? I am an architect and I would like to make it more suitable for our special situation. Gayle is concerned about

how large the kitchen is. It would require her to do a lot of walking between work areas putting undue stress on her, physically."

She said, "Modifications to the outside are not allowed. This is done to preserve the overall image of the community. However, they are allowed within reason for interior customization."

Gayle said, "I am eligible for retirement in two years. We would like to buy the house now in order to hold the lot we have selected."

Betty replied, "I am so sorry but our policy does not allow us to hold a lot for more than sixteen months to avoid the noise and dust created by construction which will disturb the neighboring houses that would be occupied by then."

Gayle said, "Can this policy be waived for a physically handicapped person like me since we need that particular lot because it is flat and would not require steps?"

Betty replied, "Please wait here while I talk to my manager. I am hoping he will find a way to get around the policy."

A short while later, she came back and informed us the lot could be held with the understanding the actual cost of the house would increase to cover inflation. She also explained that the contract would be written as if the home would be completed within the 16 month time period but we could just extend the contract at the end of that time to cover the months needed before we could actually move. We agreed to that proviso, made the required, fully refundable down payment and signed the paperwork. We now had a plan for the future and, to make it seem real, Gayle went back to the lot and picked up 3 or 4 medium rocks to take back home with us ...our small bit of Texas! We flew back to Massachusetts excited and more optimistic about the next two years. We talked about the house and the community all the way home. The next day, I looked at the plan and considered how it could be improved. I asked

Gayle what she would want if money was no object. She said that a guest bedroom would be on top of her list along with her original concern about the kitchen being too large.

Creating an extra room is quite a challenge in a small two-bedroom house since we wanted to reserve one for a home-office. I started sketching and was able to shrink the kitchen and delete a useless "formal dining room" which was only nine feet wide. This created the extra bedroom we wanted and enlarged the breakfast area. I replaced the useless and inaccessible cabinet over the refrigerator with a high window to match the one in the dining area bringing more natural light into the kitchen. I also changed the placement of the door to the second bedroom so the bathroom would be part of a bedroom suite. And I lengthened the entry hall wall to align the opening into the bedroom wing with the natural flow of traffic into the living room. This resulted in a larger and more useful hall closet. I then drew the modified plan and elevations for the new kitchen cabinets and faxed them to Betty asking her to give us a cost estimate for the modifications. A few days later, I called and she informed me that the changes would be an additional $3000.00. I expected either a rejection or a much higher figure, so we agreed, signed the paperwork for the estimate she sent and faxed it back to her. All we had to do now was wait impatiently for the two years to pass to start our new, improved lives. I knew that it cost the developer only a few hundred dollars but, to us it was a boon.

We bought a large two-year calendar, mounted it on the home-office wall and made a schedule of the steps we had to take to execute the move. We set a date for Gayle's retirement, another for putting our condo on the market and several others for the repairs that needed to be done and so on. We started fixing things such as a small crack in the basement slab, painting and caulking. On the whole, the place didn't need a lot of work. We estimated a date to contact the movers, etc. We also did the first of several reviews of the junk that inevitably accumulated over the past 14 years. We even started to pack and label boxes of records and sentimental items we knew we would not need to open until well after the move figuring every little bit done toward getting ready would be a plus. Every time we finished one of the scheduled events, we triumphantly crossed it off on the calendar.

We returned each year to visit the site as part of our vacation. This gave us a chance to get to know the community better. During one of our visits we met with one of the interior designers. She helped us choose all of the standard interior finishes from flooring, to paint colors, appliances and light fixtures. We even had to choose the color of the roofing shingles which had to conform to a coordinated set of predetermined color combinations. The number of decisions was staggering but exciting. The only choice we later changed was the color of carpet. Gayle was concerned it was much too light and would show dirt too quickly. This was easily accomplished over the phone after samples in the color range we requested arrived in the mail.

Gayle's father dies
Gayle's parents were excited when we told them we were planning to move back to Texas in the Fall of 2002. However, in February of 2001, Gayle's father Tommy's knees started to give him problems to the point he could hardly walk. He went to a doctor in Victoria (a town 35 miles south of Cuero) who performed a knee replacement operation on one of them. The operation was not very successful and caused him extreme agony. He never fully recovered from the surgery and other medical problems surfaced. He endured months of pain until

Gayle's brother, Nelson who is an attorney in Houston, finally convinced Tommy to go to a diagnostic hospital there. After running many tests, the doctor told Nelson his father had cancer which had metastasized and he had only a short time to live. Gayle and I flew from Massachusetts to Houston and stayed at a hotel until the end came. It was a very tragic time for Gayle, her brother and especially their mother. I did all I could to give my mother-in-law solace because I knew that without her husband, it seemed her world had come to an end. They had never been apart before and she did not know how to cope without him. I prayed with them and that gave them some degree of comfort.

When we later retired in Texas, I suggested to Gayle we purchase a brick engraved with Tommy's name, military rank and unit information to be placed in the Veteran's Memorial Plaza in our retirement community as a tribute to his service in WWII. She agreed and we always point it out to those who come to visit us. I miss the time we spent together playing a board game called Finger Pool. Each player would try to propel a small white wood loop to expedite his or her colored loops into the corner pocket. It was a kind of pocket pool game. Tommy was very skillful and beat us repeatedly but he did it in such a way nobody resented the fact we didn't have a chance to win against him. In spite of the fact he was a man of limited means who grew up during the depression, he had great dignity and resourcefulness that commanded respect. He never hesitated to help those who needed help. We all miss him to this day.

Gayle retires

About a year and a half after Tommy's death, when Gayle gave her four weeks notice at the Red Cross, her co-workers became very emotional upon hearing the news because she had endeared herself to everyone. She accomplished that through her sincere interactions and great sense of humor during her long employment there. At her going away party, tears were shed and her boss as well as the CEO of the New England Region paid her great compliments and handed her a certificate of appreciation. Her friends there gave her a sundial on a pedestal as a going away present to remember them by. Today, it is a nice addition to our backyard landscaping.

When it was time to put our condo on the market, we interviewed two realtors . One who charged the full going rate for handling the sale said she would post it at a price that seemed too low and we just didn't click with the other one. So we contacted a discount realtor with a company called Assist-2-Sell who was much nicer and more knowledgeable. She suggested we post it at a price that was more in line with our expectations. Gayle asked her to raise it two thousand dollars and the agent said she would do it but it might be higher than what prospective buyers would be willing to pay. Gayle held her ground because the housing market was booming and available properties located close to the commuter rail were not plentiful. She has an uncanny sense about these things.

The discount realtor did all the services a full service realtor does except show the property to prospective buyers. They list it on the multiple listing and on their web site with pictures and a full description. Our part of the deal was to show the property when she put up the open-house signs during the weekends. Gayle was a superb saleswoman. She was cheerful and frank and, in ten days, the property was sold for the asking price, more than double the price we had paid for it twelve years earlier (we had rented that unit for two years before we bought it). The movers arrived the day before we were to close on our condo. We had made reservations to stay that night and the next at a nearby hotel. After the movers left, we checked in for the evening after confirming our reservation with the auto transport company we had contacted for shipping our car the following day. Signing all the paperwork went smoothly at the attorney's office. We delivered our car to the transport company and our realtor drove us back to the hotel. We had arranged for a taxi service to pick us up the next day to make our mid-morning flight to Austin.

My nephew, Sam who, by that time, had become the owner of a major engineering firm, met us at the airport and drove us to his office where he had set aside one of his company cars for us to use until our car was delivered. He also opened his home to us for as long as we needed. We planned to stay with him just until the movers brought all our possessions to the new house. Closing on the new house was set for mid-morning the following day with the movers scheduled to arrive at 1:00 PM. We finished the walk-through tour of the house before going to the developer's office to complete all the closing papers which went smoothly. We decided to drive back by OUR HOUSE before heading to lunch. After we ate at the restaurant, we returned to the house and found, to our surprise, the movers were there ready to unload. After they put our furniture into the house and all the boxes in the garage, I started lifting some of the boxes and placing them in the rooms. After a couple of hours, we decided to call it a day because I felt tired. I asked Gayle if she could drive back to Sam's house since we had planned to stay with him and his wife Charlotte one more night. We planned to return the next day to set up the bed and make the house habitable.

That night, after we retired to the bedroom, I felt an unusual heaviness in my chest and I got up and took an aspirin thinking it would help me sleep. I ignored the chest pressure for a couple of hours more hoping it would go away. When it didn't, I told

Gayle I did not feel well and explained what I was experiencing. Gayle immediately went downstairs to tell Charlotte. We all got in her van and she headed toward Austin while telephoning a heart specialist who had treated Sam. He directed her to Seton Hospital and told her a colleague would meet us in the emergency room. As soon as we arrived there, a nurse placed a nitroglycerin pill under my tongue. I was connected to an EKG machine and blood was drawn for a heart enzyme test which later indicated I had had a mild heart attack. I was admitted and spent the night in a private room. Gayle "slept" in a chair. Charlotte stayed with us lending us a lot of support with her presence. Later that night, Sam drove about 90 miles from the conference he had attended that day to be with us. An angiogram was performed the next morning and it indicated one of the arteries located close to my heart was blocked in two places. The cardiologist performed an angioplasty, threading two stents through an artery in my groin to open the blockage.

I was kept in the ICU overnight because my blood pressure dropped during the surgery but was moved to a regular room the following morning. I was released the day after. So, spending our first night in our new house was delayed by a week. Gayle and I spent each day at the house doing light unpacking. I was restricted to lifting no more than 10 pounds and was able to help set up the kitchen in preparation to really moving in. Sam and Charlotte came with us on the weekend and set up our bed and a few days later on Halloween night 2002, Gayle and I spent our first night in our bed, under our own roof! We had made it at last!

Thankfully, I didn't experience any further heart problems. Going to the fitness center and observing a healthy diet (more or less) may have been a factor in keeping the cardiologist away. However, about two years after my heart episode occurred, we were watching TV when Gayle heard an alarming gurgling sound coming from my direction. She looked and found I had lost consciousness and continued to make that awful gurgle while my eyes rolled back in their sockets. She was terrified and called 911 telling the operator I seemed to be having a seizure. The ambulance arrived in 5 minutes. Gayle told me later it was the longest 5 minutes she had ever had to endure. She said she kept telling me to breathe! After listening to my heart and doing other checks, the EMT told her it did not seem to be any type of heart event.

While this was somewhat reassuring, that preliminary diagnosis did not explain what was wrong. They checked me for a stroke and told Gayle they did not think it was that either, since there was no evidence of any weakness. By that time I had started to stir but was not aware of what was happening, Gayle said I did not know her and just stared at her with empty eyes. The EMTs took me on a gurney to the waiting ambulance. Gayle followed the ambulance to the emergency room in our car since she needed to first gather insurance papers and get her walker to navigate the long hallways at the hospital. When she arrived, she was informed I had had a seizure but was stable. I was sent for a brain MRI and it turned out to be clear of any visible abnormalities much to our relief. In the early morning hours, the emergency room doctor recommended I see a neurologist the following day and released me to go home. By then, Sam and Charlotte had arrived and they helped Gayle by moving me from the wheelchair to the car. I was barely conscious when she drove me home because of all the muscle relaxants and other drugs that were administered at the ER. Once we drove into the garage, they got me into the house and to bed with the aid of a wheelchair we had.

The next day, we went to a neurologist recommended by my

primary care doctor. He did tests and prescribed an anti-seizure medication. That drug robbed me of my personality and aggravated my memory loss. It made me feel like a Zombie and took away any enjoyment from my existence. Anything that required the least amount of thinking was almost impossible to do. I was also told I could not drive for at least six months. The following week while working out in the yard, I had another seizure. When Gayle started looking for me, she found me on the ground between our house and our neighbor's. She went inside and phoned our neighbor for help. He is a hefty guy who could get me into the house again with the aid of the wheelchair. and got me into bed and after I fell asleep for an hour I once again regained consciousness. I went back to the neurologist for regular follow-ups and each time explained how the medication was affecting me. He prescribed a different drug. However, it too continued to make me feel as if I was sleep-walking. After enduring that condition for about a year, I rebelled and during one of my follow-up appointment, I told the doctor I was going to discontinue using the drug. He warned me that I would be taking a risk but if I was determined to get off it, he would recommend a gradual dosage reduction until I weaned myself from it.

In the meantime I was to undergo a very extensive brain study that required me to have 24 electrodes attached to my head for 48 hours to reveal any small seizures or electrical disturbances taking place without any outward symptoms. The test result was normal, so that reinforced my decision to get off the medication. It has been more than eleven years since I got off that awful medication. Thank God, I have not had any problems. It was almost a rebirth. Loss of my short-term memory is still a problem especially for names but I have my sense of humor back. Up to that time, I had been working part-time reviewing projects Fed-Exed to me from Boston. About six months after the health problems, I decided to fully retire and am enjoying my existence in this retirement heaven.

Today, we continue to live in the community and have many friends and acquaintances. We go to a Methodist church nearby where the people are very friendly and welcoming and we really like the pastor who is a wonderful preacher. We bought a new golf cart which costs little to run and does not pollute. We drive it to the fitness center, the local branch of the bank, the clinic for our doctor appointments, to our friends and, after fitting it with a second seat, it enables us to give tours to our visitors so they can enjoy watching the roaming deer. Our life could not be any more enjoyable and busy.

The Nasheds at home

CONCLUSION- Part Two

This memoir started at the back porch of our house in our retirement community where we were enjoying our coffee at dusk; I continued to think about the life which I left behind and how fortunate I have been to leave a country that didn't appreciate my value. The conditions in Egypt forced my two older brothers to emigrate before me and, thank God, all three of us have excelled in our professions despite the difficulty of functioning in a different society. We would have had no chance of achieving our goals if we had stayed. Looking back on my life after I emigrated, I find it amazing how God helped me at every turn. From the time I arrived at the airport in Austin and found a taxi driver who knew where the cheapest hotel was, to the time the Chinese student led me to an unbelievably cheap rooming house, to how He inspired Dean Taniguchi to offer me the teaching assistant job and assign me to the international competition. God enabled me to pass the professional registration test in the first try even though I was ill-prepared. He led me, to the perfect mate, gave me the ideas to write my books to cite a few of His many blessings. Without His involvement, I could have been an utter failure and may have ended on the streets. I have written this autobiography as a sort of inadequate thanks to my Savior.

Immigration is a serious step to take and must be embarked on only if conditions become exceedingly intolerable. In my case, it was well-justified because I had no control on where I worked and what I was assigned to do. The cost of living had become unsustainable and I had no opportunity to meet an eligible member of the opposite sex to give life meaning. While immigration has given me freedom and liberty, I didn't expect it to be an easy transition into my new environment. Anyone who thinks that he or she can fit right in is deluded. On the other hand, if I had remained in Egypt, I am sure that I would have either died or gone mad some time ago. I firmly believe that my pilgrimage to Jerusalem and fervent prayers to God to allow me to immigrate to the US were answered in His good time when I needed to leave so badly and had reached the point of desperation. I have found American society to be welcoming and friendly in most cases. This is a great country that acts as a beacon of hope to all the oppressed peoples of the world. I consider myself most fortunate to have been allowed to live here. The potential for professional progress and financial independence is limitless and the standard of living is very high in comparison to the one I left behind. It is true that I had some negative experiences in North Carolina but even there, we had enjoyable occasions when we visited the impressive Vanderbilt mansion in Asheville and took drives in the Smoky Mountains. Some of the negative experiences I had on this side of the Atlantic were probably partly caused by me through misunderstandings.

America is one of the few countries that welcomes legal immigrants with open arms, offers them employment based on ability and not on religious belief or ethnic background. Most of the citizens are descended from immigrants and welcome new ones. Of course there are rednecks but they are a small minority. In this country, one can pick up and leave a job, a city or even a state, if conditions get to be unfavorable. To me this freedom is priceless. Another advantage of living in the US is that bribery is not condoned. In third world countries, bribery, graft and corruption are the norm. I could never get myself to bribe anyone in Egypt and that made life rather difficult. One of the reasons I abstained from that practice is one never knew if the person accepting the bribe worked for the secret police. We Americans, native-born and legal immigrants, must not take our freedoms and all the gifts that this wonderful country has bestowed on us for granted so that this country may continue to be that famous beacon on a hill that President Reagan cited in one of his memorable speeches. This autobiography was partly written to express my deepest thanks to my God and my adopted country.

* * *

After spending a whole year writing, adding, rewriting and refining this manuscript, I was surprised to find out that Gayle decided to write a foreword. After I read it, I was overcome by the depth of feeling that this amazing woman has shown in those few paragraphs, a feeling and style that put to shame what I had tried to express in a whole book of illustrated prose describing my whole life and the life of my family. I feel truly blessed to have been led to share my undeserving life with that dear woman.

Fred Nashea

ABOUT THE AUTHOR

Fred Nashed graduated from the School of Fine Arts in Cairo, Egypt with a degree in architecture in 1952. He received an MA degree from the School of Architecture at the University of Texas in 1975. During his study there, he worked as a Teaching Assistant, his entry in an international competition to upgrade slums in developing nations was chosen to represent the university. His career included design and construction of major projects at firms in Egypt, Texas, North Carolina and Boston. In 1994, he established a consulting firm performing the final technical and coordination checks on projects for some of the major firms in Boston until he retired and returned to Texas in 2002.

He authored three technical books, two were published by McGraw-Hill in 1996 and 2009 and the third by Van Nostrand Reinhold in 1993. One of the books was translated to Chinese. He also presented well-attended seminars for architects and engineers at the Build Boston symposia. He has been married to Gayle, a wonderful fellow student from UT for the past 44 years and currently resides in an active adult retirement community in Texas. Disney World is their favorite vacation spot and they try to go there every year.

9 781364 659837